IMAGES
of America

MORIAH AND PORT HENRY IN THE ADIRONDACKS

WOMEN IN THE MINES, C. 1944. Throughout the history of Port Henry and Moriah, women have played essential roles as administrators, teachers, business leaders, and historians. This photograph shows wives of miners and female employees of Republic Steel visiting the mines. They wear hard hats and headlamps and sit in one of the tramcars that took miners down into the shafts. There are many photographs of the men who worked in the mines, but this is one of the few of the women who contributed to the work of the mines. (Courtesy of the Town of Moriah Historical Society.)

ON THE COVER: The First Presbyterian Church has stood for more than 120 years at the corner of Main and Church Streets in downtown Port Henry. In this view from about 1895, the congregation has come outside to pose on the front lawn and under the porte cochere, the covered stone archway where people could step out of carriages. Young children and adults of all ages are gathered here. Today, this church is known as Mount Moriah Presbyterian. (Courtesy of the Town of Moriah Historical Society.)

IMAGES
of America

MORIAH AND PORT HENRY IN THE ADIRONDACKS

Jacqueline A. Viestenz and
Frank Edgerton Martin
Foreword by Joan Crawford Daby

ARCADIA
PUBLISHING

Published by Arcadia Publishing
Charleston, South Carolina

Library of Congress Control Number: 2012947186

For all general information, please contact Arcadia Publishing:
Telephone 843-853-2070
Fax 843-853-0044
E-mail sales@arcadiapublishing.com
For customer service and orders:
Toll-Free 1-888-313-2665

Visit us on the Internet at www.arcadiapublishing.com

To all of the miners and their families

CONTENTS

FOREWORD

The majority of photographs used in this book come from our Town of Moriah Historical Society and Historian archives. We thank all the wonderful people who so generously donated them or allowed us to copy them over the years so that they may be used to keep our local history alive. This is why the Town of Moriah Historical Society was organized in 1992.

When I became the town and village of Port Henry historian, I put out a feeler to see if there was an interest in forming a historical society. Special interest in the history of Witherbee, Sherman & Company, the Republic Steel Corporation, and the Lake Champlain & Moriah Railroad Company made it happen in November 1992. Since then, we have shared our historical findings with the public by way of our yearly Historic Moriah Calendars, through presentations of a historical nature by several people, and by displaying our historical artifacts and photographs in the Iron Center interpretive museum and our Historian and Research Rooms in Port Henry. Also, I have published historical articles in the *Times of Ti*, Ticonderoga's newspaper, to spark interest in our local history.

Our community was built around the lumbering, farming, and iron industries so many years ago. Now, with modern technology, our story is being told around the world using photographs and text by way of the Internet.

—Joan Crawford Daby
Town of Moriah Historian Emeritus

ACKNOWLEDGMENTS

It takes many hands to make a book. This one would not have been possible without the help of Joan Daby and Betty LaMoria, who opened the Moriah Historical Society's rich archives for our use. They provided invaluable advice in identifying photographs and recommending subjects that we should explore.

We are also grateful to Archie Rosenquist for sharing his knowledge of the mining operations in Moriah. Peggy Porter, Anna Beebe, and Mary Consadine all shared remarkable photographs and printed items from their personal collections. Deborah Henry, Bernadette Trow, and Dorothy Baxter Wilber also shared images. Janet Beebe Denney photographed contemporary views of our community. Sarah Tichonuk, who has many talents as a historian and graphic designer, scanned nearly every image in this book. John Viestenz provided his sharp eyes to editing the text. We are deeply grateful to all of these supporters and to everyone else who has given us a word of encouragement along the way.

Unless otherwise noted, all of the photographs in this book are from the Town of Moriah Historical Society archives.

INTRODUCTION

In the late 1800s, Port Henry and the surrounding town of Moriah lay at the forefront of emerging American wealth, industrial power, and technological prowess. Moriah supplied much of the rich iron needed to build the cannons, ships, and guns used by the Union in the Civil War. In the ensuing decades, the founders and executives from Witherbee, Sherman & Company built grand houses and churches, laid out gazebos and elegant gardens, and supported retail businesses. The lives of the miners who worked for them were far less affluent, and their work was far more dangerous. However, these extremes of wealth led to some of the most diverse and varied architecture in New York State.

The town of Moriah was famed throughout the metallurgical world for its iron mines, which can be traced back to the Revolutionary War. The product of the mines was shipped to nearly every iron-making center in this country and Canada. The ore was of varied quality, so almost any character of iron could be made from them. The ore averaged about 63 percent in iron and between 30 and 40 percent in phosphorus.

The mines had several owners through the years. The Port Henry Iron Ore Company was organized in 1864. Witherbee, Sherman & Company bought the mines in 1900. Republic Steel Corporation leased the Mineville operations in 1938 until their closing in 1971. This book opens with a remarkable collection of photographs of the mining operations from 1870 to 1970. During the Civil War, Moriah provided much of the ore for the Union effort, including the iron for the famed ironclad surface warship *Monitor*. Moriah's mines supported American industry in World War II through vast expansion of output and the construction of two entirely new villages to house workers, including Grover Hills, which still stands today. In the opening chapter, we visit this now largely lost landscape of mine shafts, iron ore separators, tailings piles, blast furnaces, miner rescue squads, and more recent portraits of retired miners.

Throughout its history, Witherbee, Sherman & Company founded civic institutions that made Port Henry and surrounding villages model communities. Company leaders subsidized public amenities such as golf courses, seminaries, parks, and cemeteries. The result is that Port Henry is home to a stunning collection of architectural styles in local landmarks, including the Sherman Free Library, the First National Bank (today's Glens Falls National Bank), Mount Moriah Presbyterian Church, and the Moriah Town Hall, formerly the headquarters of Witherbee, Sherman & Company.

Through high-quality historical photographs and postcards, this book explores these gardens, churches, libraries, and community halls. A separate chapter documents the two company towns, Witherbee and Mineville. Witherbee, Sherman & Company engineered in-house structures to meet new early-1900s worker safety laws. As rare examples of construction made entirely of block using mining tailings, the villages of Witherbee and Mineville offer a wealth of photography, showing streets, stores, row houses, and vistas of tailings piles with mountain landscapes and Lake Champlain in the distance.

Port Henry is also home to one of the nation's oldest diners. Dating from 1926 and built by the Ward & Dickinson Company of Silver Creek, New York, this patented model predates many of the sleek metal diners found across New England. With a raised monitor roof like an old train car, Port Henry's diner still has the wheels that were used to transport it from the factory to its intended site.

Another fascinating story is Port Henry's role in the silent film industry. Opened in the mid-1920s, Arctic City Film Studios produced many Klondike gold rush pictures involving dog teams, imperiled maidens, and snowy mountain scenes. Drawing noted actors such as Pearl White and Francis X. Bushman, Port Henry was the perfect base for filming this vision of the exotic north. This book contains several historical images of the actors, a recreated Wild West town, and images from film production.

Moriah and the village of Port Henry have long traditions of civic pride and recreation, with events in all four seasons ranging from hunting to sailing. This book features photographs of Labor Day parades, ice fishing, skiing, baseball games, and Johnny Podres, the celebrated left-handed pitcher and Moriah native who helped lead the Brooklyn Dodgers to their historic 1955 World Series victory.

In a northern mountain community with dangerous mining operations, citizens have long volunteered in fire departments, mine rescue squads, maritime rescue teams, and as emergency medical technicians. We document these groups through portraits, images of evolving equipment, and the proud role that they take in marching in annual parades, especially at Labor Day.

Lake Champlain's rich maritime history is documented through images of steamers, ferry boats, barges, yachts, sailboats, and other vessels. The original 1929 Champlain Bridge was demolished in 2009. In 2011, the arch for the new bridge was constructed on the lakefront in Port Henry and then floated down the lake for integration into the new structure. The dramatic summer event took place just a few days before the onslaught of Hurricane Irene.

As one of the closest New York communities to this important bridge, Port Henry is located on Route 9N, a historic road that has linked New York City and Montreal for more than 200 years. Today, Port Henry's Main Street and Route 9N are part of the Lakes to Locks Scenic Byway, a tourist and cultural route that surrounds Lake Champlain and attracts many driving tourists, bicyclists, and weekend visitors. From Memorial Day through the fall leaf season, thousands of people pass through Moriah on Route 9N. They stop for camping, tours of Port Henry's Iron History Museum, hiking, and other attractions. How many communities lie at the foot of a great mountain range like the Adirondacks, look over one of the most historic lakes in North America, and tell a story of the rise of American industry over the last two centuries? This book is a visual guide to the generations of immigrants and longtime residents whose hard work and creativity built one of New York's most fascinating regions.

One

NEW YORK'S IRON CAPITAL

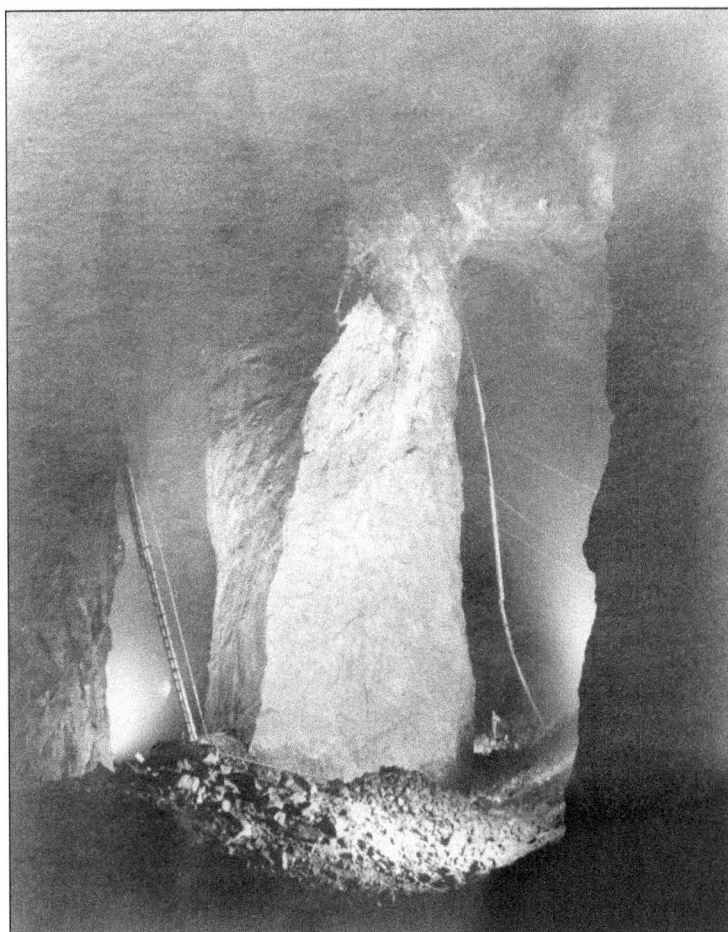

MAGNETITE PILLAR, c. 1945. This dramatically lit view in the Clonan Shaft shows a supporting pillar of magnetite ore. It was blasted by first cutting off the top and preparing the "roof" for safety. Then, 13 diamond drill holes were cut vertically down into the 150-foot pillar. For a sense of the huge scale of this space, look closely at the lower-right base of the column and the tiny figure of a man bathed in the spotlights.

CHEEVER MINE, C. 1875. Named for Dr. Abijah Cheever, the Cheever ore bed was the oldest working mine in Moriah. As early as 1760, there are accounts of ore cropping out on the surface. During the Revolutionary War, Cheever supplied ore for the Colonial forges at Whitehall. Formal mining did not begin until 1804, with several different owners subsequently mining there. With ore of great purity, the Cheever product required minimal separating.

359. Iron Works, Port Henry, N. Y.

BAY STATE FURNACE. The Bay State Furnace, shown here around 1867, was built on the site of the region's first blast furnace, which was built by Maj. James Dalliba in the mid-1820s. Before rail service became available in 1869, ore was transported to Dalliba's furnace by wagon from the Cheever bed and Dalliba bed, which was later known as the Lee Mine. Velez Marina currently occupies the site.

THE IRON MINE. This oil canvas of Port Henry's mine was painted by Homer Dodge Martin in 1862. Martin's celebrated painting of the Cragg Harbor's horizontal mine shafts hangs prominently in the Smithsonian Museum of American Art. Born in Albany in 1836, Martin traveled to the Catskills and the Adirondacks to paint the majestic mountain scenes. Visible from Lake Champlain, their mine was ideally located for shipments by water to the furnaces in Port Henry and, ultimately, down the Hudson River to New York City. Steam power was used to hoist the ore to the railroad. The iron ore bed at Cragg Harbor was a source for much of the Union's iron during the Civil War. As a Union supporter, it is likely that Martin painted these mines to show the industrial resources and prowess of the North. During the Civil War, Moriah iron would contribute to the construction of Union cannons, cannonballs, and even the famed ironclad surface warship *Monitor*. (Courtesy of Smithsonian American Art Museum, gift of William T. Evans.)

THE 21 MINE. The 21 Mine was begun in 1829. In 1877, it was transformed into a 300-foot-deep open-pit mine. The hoisting system of an inclined skip way and two cableways allowed for a large tonnage of ore to be extracted at an extremely low cost. A hoist room and tracks going underground were installed in 1906. The 21 Mine continued to operate until 1924.

JOKER SHAFT WITH STORAGE BINS. The Joker shaft was sunk in the 1880s. The depth to reach ore was deeper than expected and thus the shaft was named Joker. In the 1880s and 1890s, there were two skip ways in the shaft. The storage bins shown here each held 1,000 tons of ore. The shaft was in the vicinity of the Don B. shaft, between Memorial Hall and the change room.

GROUP OF MINERS, C. 1940. For generations, Port Henry and Moriah was one of the most diverse communities in upstate New York. This photograph of miners shows their sense of camaraderie in the face of danger and hard work. Most of Moriah's miners were first- or second-generation immigrants from Hungary, Poland, Ireland, and Italy. Many of them, and almost all of their parents, still spoke with strong accents from their native lands. There were also dozens of African American families who lived throughout Moriah and Port Henry and stayed for generations. Older residents recall that there was a great sense of acceptance for all ethnicities during the mining years because they were all, in many ways, outsiders and newcomers to the American Dream.

MINE RESCUE TEAM, C. 1940. These are the brave men who went down in the mines to rescue their comrades when there was an accident. Here, an instructor from the Bureau of Mines (left), has just finished conducting a mock rescue to train the men for a real event.

1500 LEVEL DRILL REPAIR SHOP. Repair shops were located underground so that drills and other equipment could be repaired more efficiently. Here, from left to right, Homer Mathews, Bill Anderson, Ray Pickern, Earl "Bud" Haseltine, Arnold Conley, and John "Shorty" Dereski review the orders for the work that needs to be done. (Courtesy of the Bill Anderson collection.)

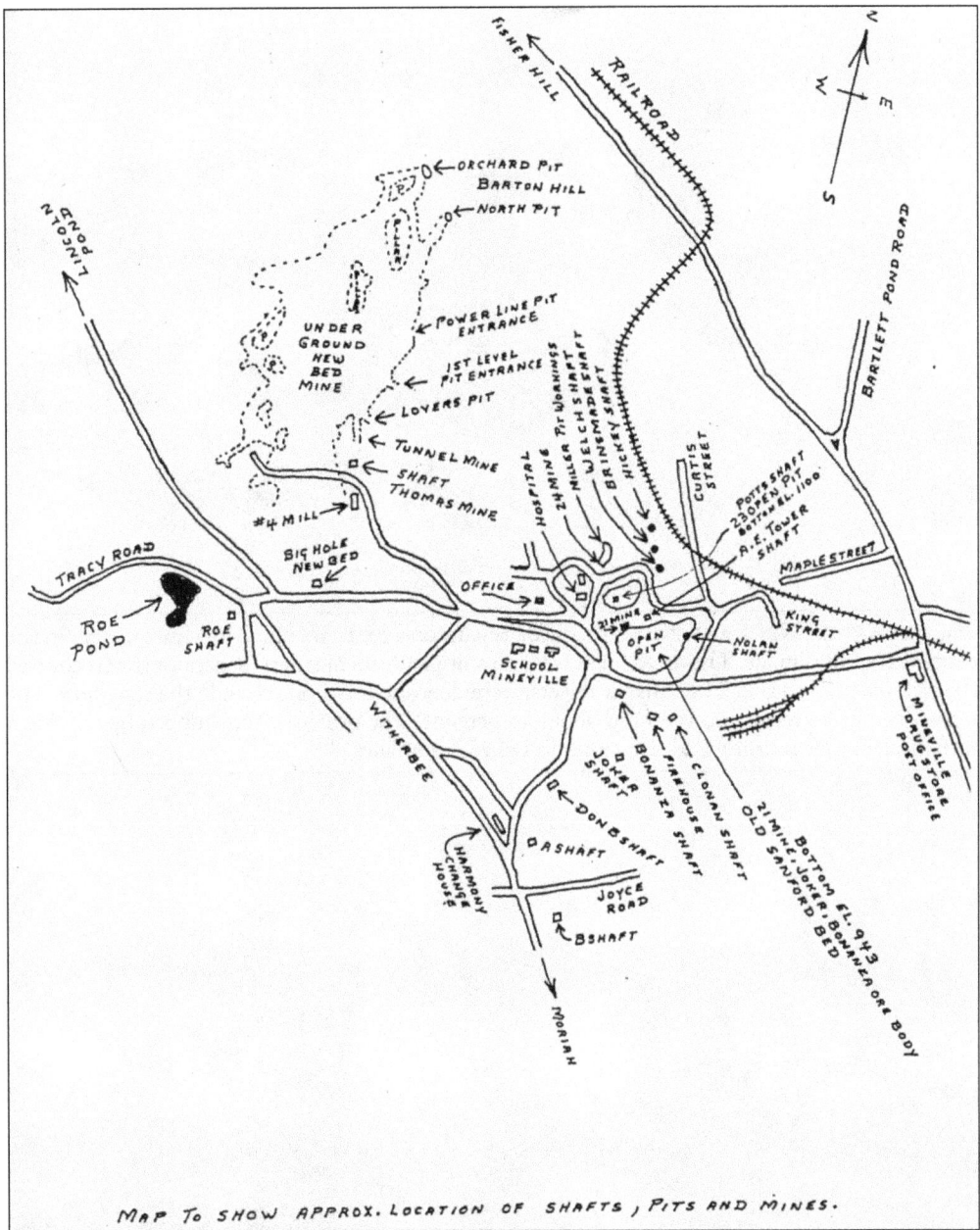

MAP TO SHOW APPROX. LOCATION OF SHAFTS, PITS AND MINES.

DRAWING OF MINE LOCATIONS. This map, probably drawn by a miner from memory, shows the location of the mines in Mineville. The 21 Mine, the open-pit mine in the center, was the oldest mine. Joker shaft and the Bonanza mine, just south of the 21 Mine, were opened in the 1880s. Clonan shaft opened in 1908–1909. The Harmony and Joker shafts produced the purest magnetite ore, requiring minimal processing. The lives of the miners who worked in these locations were hard and sometimes dangerous. Before Republic Steel took over the mines, safety conditions were more lax. In those early years, miners wore soft hats and carbide lamps. After 1938, safety improvements were made, and men began to wear hard hats and battery lamps. The mines employed many immigrants, including Polish, Italian, and German men. Safety and directional signs underground were printed in several languages.

ORE SEPARATORS NO. 1 AND NO. 2, C. 1920. Separators No. 1 and No. 2 in Mineville are in the center left of this image. The dried ore was fed to a single-drum magnetic separator that recovered the rich particles of ore. The tails, or rejects, were deposited in a pile outside the separator. The iron concentrate recovered averaged about 65 percent. The ore was then shipped by rail down to Port Henry for refining and shipment on Lake Champlain.

MILL NO. 3. The No. 3 Ore Separator, or mill, processed iron ore to a uniform size to suit customer requirements. The No. 3 Mill was built in 1910 between the Harmony A and B shafts. Its close proximity was in order to minimize the distance required to convey heavy ore. This processor was destroyed by fire in 1922. (Courtesy of the Sherman Free Library.)

MILL NO. 4 AND TAILINGS PILE, C. 1910 POSTCARD. The substantial tailings pile that resulted from the separation of the rich iron ore from the bedrock is seen in this postcard. Mill No. 4 used safer equipment than the previous mills and operated with more efficiency.

MILL NO. 7, C. 1944. This mill was at the change house near #7 Mill and at the switchback. This photograph also shows piles of sized rock and conveyors for the asphalt plant. The ore was fed by conveyor belt to high-intensity wet magnetic separators. The iron ore was then passed over several screens to separate the rock into different sizes. The tailings were discharged to a waste tailings area. The concrete silos seen here housed different sizes of crushed rock; some of this crushed rock would eventually be used to build roads.

POWER PLANT, C. 1915 POSTCARD. Witherbee, Sherman & Company built this state-of-the-art power plant to supply electricity to the mining operations and AC power for the homes and businesses of Port Henry. Built in 1908 on the lakefront below their headquarters, the power plant was sited for easy coal delivery by barge. The power plant closed in 1922.

TRAVELING CRANE, C. 1910 POSTCARD. At one time, there were 20 railroad sidings to accommodate the ore cars that were transported from Port Henry to all parts of the country. The traveling crane took the processed ore from the trestle and deposited it in the railcars or on barges or canal boats. The crane used magnets to lift the ore and deposit it in the cars for shipment.

FIRST CEDAR POINT FURNACE, C. 1890. The first Cedar Point Furnace was built under the direction of Thomas F. Witherbee in 1872–1874 and operated from 1875 to 1924. Witherbee installed the first Whitwell firebrick stoves ever erected in this country. He also introduced his invention of the Witherbee bronze tuyeres, or pipes. The Lake Champlain & Moriah Railroad took ore from the mines to the furnace. Coal for the furnace was delivered by canal boat and later by the New York & Canada Railroad. Tailings from the furnace were dumped along the lakeshore, creating a landfill area of several hundred feet.

NEW CEDAR POINT FURNACE. Cedar Point Furnace No. 2 was built in 1922. Earl Henry supervised the construction, and its design was considered the "last word" in furnace construction and efficiency. Ultimately, the new furnace's debt costs challenged Witherbee, Sherman & Company. The furnace only operated until 1924, closing due to a slumping economy and growing competition from Midwestern mines. Henry's oldest son, Lowell, supervised its demolition in 1939. (Courtesy of the Sherman Free Library.)

GIANT PIECE OF ORE, C. 1940. This is the largest piece of magnetite ore ever mined from the operations of Republic Steel in Moriah. It was discovered in 1940 and is seen here resting on a lifting device with a miner standing nearby to provide a sense of scale. The ore was displayed throughout the East Coast.

ELECTRIC SCRAPER AND OPERATOR. This "hoe-type" scraper was developed in Mineville in the 1920s. It consisted of 60-inch curved manganese steel plates with reinforced scraping edges so the blade could be reversed. It was used to hoist sections of rock to a higher level. (Courtesy of Moriah Historical Society, donated by Marilyn Rodick.)

MINEVILLE OPERATIONS, C. 1935. This commercial photograph documents part of Witherbee, Sherman & Company's complex operations in Mineville in the 1930s. The lower buildings in the foreground are the shaft houses for the Joker, Bonanza, and Clonan mine shafts. In the rear, the tall angled structures are Mill No. 1 and Mill No. 2. The Lake Champlain & Moriah Railroad weaves through the processors to pick up ore for shipment. The Clonan shaft was named for E.P. Clonan, a longtime supervisor of the mines.

Mineville Tailings Pile. A huge tailings pile developed from the operations of the mines. Conveyors brought the tailings from Mill No. 7 and deposited them on the pile. This pile is still a landmark in Moriah and visible from several miles away. The tailings pile contains 12.5 million tons of material. In 1986, the property was sold to Rhone-Poulenc, Inc., a large producer of rare earth minerals owned by the French government.

PUBLIC MEETING

VILLAGE SQUARE

PORT HENRY, N. Y.

THURS., MARCH 28th
2 P. M.

Come and hear Joseph T. McNichols, Director of the United Steelworkers of America CIO, Dist. 3.

If you want the Truth about the Labor situation and not warped Corporation Propaganda

ATTEND!!

Flier for 1946 Union Strike. The American Federation of Labor (AFL) represented the mine workers in the 1940s. In 1945, the Congress of Industrial Organizations (CIO) sent organizers to Mineville. A National Labor Relations Board election was held, and the CIO won by a large majority. In 1946, the workers demanded and finally received a wage increase of 18.5¢ per hour.

24

INSTALLING TRACKS, 1917. The railroad was an essential component of the mining operation. It carried the raw ore from Mineville to Port Henry for processing. The Lake Champlain & Moriah Railroad, with its special steam engines, ore cars, and steep grades, offered a challenge to young men. They started as laborers and hoped to become brakemen, firemen, conductors, and finally, engineers. These men install new tracks by the Fisher Hill mine in 1917.

LAKE CHAMPLAIN & MORIAH RAILROAD OVERPASS, C. 1910. The LC&M Railroad was chartered in 1867 and built shortly thereafter. It originally traveled west on the north side of the brook on Whitney Street to what was called Terio's Wye, which was actually a switchback. This would continue until 1909, when the two overpasses and a horseshoe curve were constructed.

DONKEY ENGINE. The small donkey engine was used in the rail yard for switching rolling stock. In the background is a pile of pig iron, which was made by forming ingots at right angles to a channel or a runner. The result is a configuration that resembles a litter of piglets suckling, thus the name. After the metal hardened, the "pigs" were broken from the runner.

CABOOSE, C. 1940. This caboose operated for many years on the Lake Champlain & Moriah (LCMR) trains that hauled ore from the Mineville operations down to Port Henry. The caboose is now restored as part of a larger LCMR train located near the Port Henry railroad station and the Moriah Town Hall, formerly the headquarters of Witherbee, Sherman & Company. (Courtesy of the Anna Beebe collection.)

DOWNTOWN RAILROAD OVERPASSES, C. 1920. The Lake Champlain & Moriah Railroad crossed Route 9N on its way to the Port Henry blast furnaces. Workers going to the mines could wait at the shelter building on the right for the train to take them to Mineville. After their shifts, they could take the train back to Port Henry to the station. This trestle no longer exists. (Courtesy of the Sherman Free Library.)

WITHERBEE, SHERMAN & COMPANY HEADQUARTERS. Park Street lives up to it name, as it is the entry to a lovely park that slopes down to the Port Henry railroad station from the Witherbee, Sherman & Company headquarters. Looking west away from Lake Champlain, this view shows the fine elm trees that once lined the street anda couple of other buildings that are no longer there.

SUPPORTERS OF THE IRON CENTER. On August 20, 1998, the Moriah community opened the Iron Center Interpretive Museum with the help of dedicated citizens. Located in the former carriage house of the Witherbee, Sherman & Company headquarters, the Iron Center is a unique Lake Champlain attraction covering mining history. Retired miners have contributed their oral histories and guide visitors through the exhibits. Seen here are, from left to right, former Moriah town supervisor Dominic Ida and retired miners Louis Velsini, Martin Bezon, and Bob Carpenter, who were all major contributors to the Iron Center's opening.

21 MINE. It is hard to grasp the scale in this photograph of the 21 Mine, with its various shafts cut into the rock wall; but, toward the horizon are three tall, angled head houses of other mines, with the Adirondacks in the far background.

Two

IRON WEALTH AND INSTITUTION BUILDING

SHERMAN PARK, C. 1910 POSTCARD. John R. Sherman built this Tudor-style mansion on Broad Street overlooking Port Henry. This view shows the entry drive with its evenly spaced trees. Sherman ultimately left his estate to the Sisters of St. Joseph to be used as a girls' academy for high school–level instruction. The stone gates and part of the house still survive.

VILLAGE HALL, PORT HENRY, C. 1908 POSTCARD. Built at the height of the iron-mining boom and damaged by arson in 1933, Port Henry's monumental Village Hall stood on the same site as today's smaller replacement, built in 1941. Behind the building is the "fly space" for the sets of theater productions in the auditorium. Note the detailed Corinthian-style columns and pilasters on the porch and on the corners of the facade.

CITIZENS NATIONAL BANK OF PORT HENRY, C. 1910 POSTCARD. Shaped like a classical treasure box with a dome on top, the Citizens Bank of Port Henry (now Glens Falls National Bank) is a superb example of the Georgian Revival style popular in the early 1900s. When visiting, note the cornerstone with the date of construction, 1908, and the quality of the paneling and cabinetry inside. The former Village Hall stands to the left in this postcard. (Courtesy of the Anna Beebe collection.)

GRADUATES FROM SHERMAN PARK SEMINARY, C. 1920. John R. Sherman left his hilltop estate to the Sisters of St. Joseph, who founded a high school and seminary for girls in 1913. With both local students and boarding students from around the northeast, Sherman Park Seminary was widely respected for its Catholic and liberal arts education for girls in grades 9 through 12. This photograph shows an early graduating class sitting in their caps and silk gowns on Sherman Park's porch. They were likely exceptionally well educated for young women of the time, and several of them may have continued on to college. Large ferns fan out in the background, and each of the graduates holds a bouquet. Sherman Park centered around the large Tudor-style mansion with porches and a covered carriage entrance. Today, some of the estate's outbuildings and part of the original house remain. Trees have grown up to obscure the once sweeping view of Lake Champlain.

NEW TRAIN DEPOT IN PORT HENRY, C. 1895. The prosperity from iron mining brought many impressive public buildings to Port Henry, including the train depot. Built in 1888 for the Delaware & Hudson rail line, the depot is Richardsonian Romanesque in style. Its arched windows, shingled gables, and angled cupola are superb examples of design and craftsmanship. The expense of the materials and the intricate quality of the design attest to the importance of Port Henry at the time. Witherbee, Sherman & Company occasionally commissioned special trains to bring investors and business partners directly to Port Henry for meetings and mine tours. These photographs were taken by W.H. Bigalow, a professional photographer who worked in Port Henry for several decades around 1900. The depot is still in use today for the Amtrak Adirondack line, connecting New York City and Montreal. The depot is also home to the Senior Citizen Center of Port Henry. Volunteer seniors help passengers meet the daily northbound and southbound trains in the image below.

PORT HENRY SCHOOL BUILDING, C. 1900 POSTCARD. This three-story brick building, with its wooden cupola rising at the center of the hipped roof, rivaled nearby churches in height. Built in 1866, Port Henry's grand school building was originally known as the Union Free Academy. The school first served as an academy for training teachers. Demolished in 1916, the building was replaced with a new high school, pictured below.

NEW PORT HENRY HIGH SCHOOL, C. 1920. Once a proud civic landmark at the end of Church Street, Port Henry's new high school's opening was delayed due to the Spanish flu epidemic of 1917–1918. The stone and brick building had a "Girls" front entrance to the right and a "Boys" entrance on the left. Home to the "Orange and Black," Port Henry High School closed in 1967 after the creation of Moriah Central School. The empty building burned in 2003.

SAINT PATRICK'S CHURCH, C. 1900. Port Henry and Moriah are home to many generations of Catholics. For more than a century, Saint Patrick's has been a spiritual home for hundreds of families of French-Canadian, Polish, Italian, and Hungarian descent. Today, the church remains a vital community center with rich music, social service, education, and worship programs. Note the parish house on the left, which no longer stands.

Episcopal Church, Port Henry, N. Y.

CHRIST EPISCOPAL CHURCH, C. 1900. After its founding in the 1840s, Christ Episcopal Church opened this ornate new building in 1872 on Henry Street. Rev. William Reed Woodbridge served as its first rector until his "removal" to Brooklyn in 1898. Over the next century, about 20 different ministers served the church, which operated until 1993. The high-style Carpenter Gothic wooden building still stands today.

FIRST METHODIST CHURCH, C. 1940 DRAWING. The First Methodist Church and Mount Moriah Presbyterian Church were neighbors on the appropriately named Church Street. Both continue as churches today, although the Methodist church in this note card closed in the 1990s. Built in 1872, the venerable redbrick building is now home to the Lake Champlain Bible Fellowship. Recently, volunteer workers restored the roof, windows, and walls to their original grandeur.

MOUNT MORIAH PRESBYTERIAN CHURCH, C. 1910 POSTCARD. Built with financial support from the Witherbee family in the late 1800s, Mount Moriah Presbyterian Church (below) reflects the Romanesque style popularized by such architects as H.H. Richardson of Boston. Also seen on the cover of this book, the church is an American impression of Roman arches and engineering. The curving porte cochere still has high steps to accommodate visitors stepping out of horse-drawn carriages.

Methodist Episcopal Church
Port Henry, N.Y.

PRESBYTERIAN CHURCH, PORT HENRY, N.Y.

SHERMAN FREE LIBRARY, C. 1920 POSTCARD. Designed by architect S. Gifford Slocum of Saratoga Springs, the Sherman Free Library's slate roofs, portico arch, and semicircular window transoms express the high style of English Victorian elegance. Building styles are often hybrids and can be difficult to define—interestingly, when the library opened in January 1887, the *New York Times* described it as "Gothic." (Courtesy of the Anna Beebe collection.)

CHAMPLAIN ACADEMY, C. 1900 POSTCARD. Founded as a convent and a Catholic school, the Champlain Academy stood for generations on Highway 9N in the area known locally as Convent Hill. Three elegant arches adorned the front porch facing towards Lake Champlain. To the south, another porch overlooked an enclosed garden. (Courtesy of the Anna Beebe collection.)

INTERIOR OF SHERMAN FREE LIBRARY, C. 1975. The Sherman Free Library looks much the same today as it did when it was built. The interior has two large quarter-sawn oak tables, wooden Doric columns, and beaded board walls and ceilings. Looking up, the high-coved ceilings resemble the inside of an old wooden boat. There are original paintings, sculptures, and historical maps on view. Built in 1887 with funds donated from George Riley Sherman, the library includes many historical albums, postcards, and books about the Adirondack region. There are also extensive holdings on the Civil War. The library was later expanded to the rear in 1907. At its founding, Sherman created an endowment of $10,000 to be used to maintain the library. In 1901, the library received a further endowment of $10,000 from the will of his widow, Jane H. Sherman. The library is currently supported by interest from the Sherman Trust, the Town of Moriah, the Village of Port Henry, annual fundraising, and the Clinton-Essex-Franklin Library System. (Courtesy of the Sherman Free Library.)

MEMORIAL HALL IN MINEVILLE, C. 1910. Located at the heart of the Witherbee, Sherman & Company mining operations, Memorial Hall remains one of the greatest architectural legacies of the mine operators. Built in the Romanesque shingle style as a community center for company employees and their families, Memorial Hall (now the VFW) includes a banquet hall, meeting rooms, ballrooms, and a bowling alley, all of which are still open to the public.

WITHERBEE, SHERMAN & COMPANY OFFICES, C. 1900 POSTCARD. Built in the 1874 as the headquarters of Witherbee, Sherman & Company, this Second Empire structure with its center cupola is now Moriah's town hall. Next door, the second floor of the Italianate-style carriage house was originally used as a mineral testing laboratory, an advanced application of technology for the time. Today, the carriage house is home to the Iron Center Interpretive Museum and the Moriah Historical Society.

Three

FIRE DEPARTMENTS

PORT HENRY FIREHOUSE, C. 1890. Built in 1883 with funds donated by W.S. Sherman, Port Henry's original firehouse survives today as a residence and is listed in the National Register of Historic Places. This early group of firemen stands in one of the angle-door bays, proudly showing off their steam engine boiler and hand-sewn uniforms.

EARLY FIRE DEPARTMENT AT NEW FIREHOUSE, c. 1890. Standing proudly in front of their modern facility, these 15 firefighters pose for a portrait. It was likely a warm summer day, as most of the doors and windows of the firehouse stand open for breezes. Originally, the facade boasted a rounded parapet topped by a hipped-roofed tower. Note the balance of angled and curved doors. (Courtesy of the Sherman Free Library.)

1908 INSPECTION DAY, PORT HENRY. In the early 1900s, many New York towns celebrated Inspection Day to honor firefighters. In Port Henry, the village board visited the firehouse on Broad Street once each year to inspect the fire engines and facilities. After the inspection, the all-volunteer company proudly marched through downtown displaying its horses and equipment. Here, crowds gather in the street as the town band prepares to play from the bandstand.

FIRE DEPARTMENT AT THE PRESBYTERIAN CHURCH, C. 1895. This fascinating photograph shows 16 members of the fire department dressed in their formal garb and posing before the covered archway of the First Presbyterian Church (now the Mount Moriah Presbyterian Church). The firemen stand holding bouquets as if for a special occasion. In the center of the men, a cart with fire hoses is bedecked with flowers. At the rear, a young girl wearing a head wreath sits prominently in a white dress. Behind her, American flags are draped as a backdrop. It is likely that this photograph was taken just before or after a parade for Labor Day or Inspection Day. The pretty girl was probably the star of their float. Perhaps, a grateful village gave the firefighters the flowers in appreciation. Their white gloves highlight the sharp design of their suits and caps.

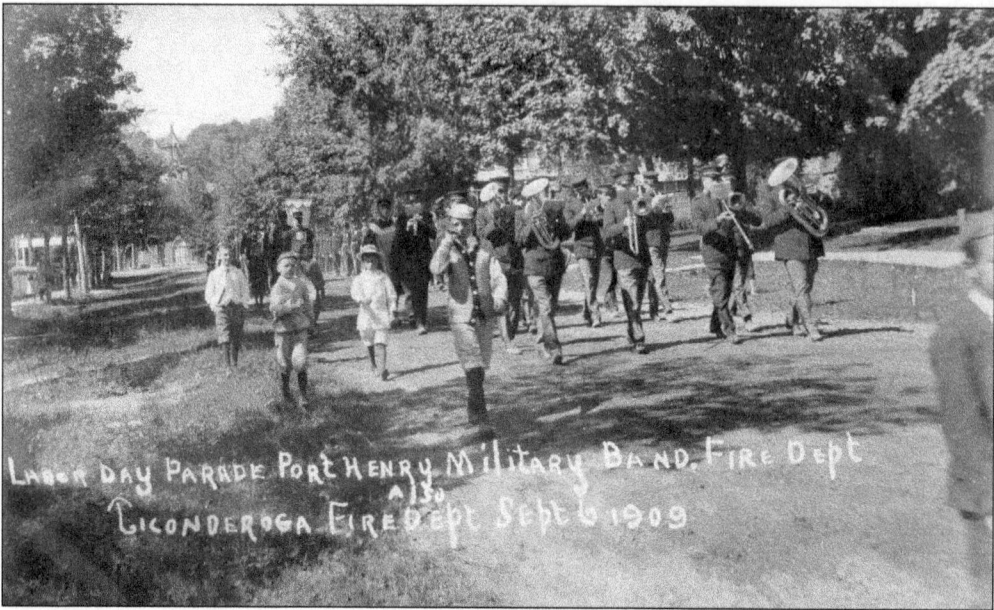

FIRE DEPARTMENTS ON PARADE, C. 1900. The Labor Day parades drew spectators from surrounding communities, and the fire departments from Crown Point, Ticonderoga, and Elizabethtown sent their finest equipment for the parade. Men from several fire departments donned their finest uniforms and marched in the parade. (Courtesy of the Sherman Free Library.)

PORT HENRY FIRE DEPARTMENT, C. 1950. Port Henry had a large volunteer fire department throughout the early and mid-1900s. Here, firemen pose on the steps of an unknown courthouse in their belted uniforms. It is interesting to note how their uniforms evolved over the generations, from the braided suits of the 1800s to a more modern, somewhat military look.

Four

Downtown Port Henry Through the Decades

BROAD STREET LOOKING EAST, C. 1890. After the building boom of the 1870s and 1880s, Port Henry was one of the largest towns on Lake Champlain. This view shows the Lewald Opera House, opened in 1874, the Van Ornam & Murdock Block, and the Lee House hotel, to the right. Note that the roads are still gravel and that new street trees have been recently planted to the left.

MAIN STREET LOOKING NORTH, C. 1905. Before the automobile, downtown Port Henry was home to several livery stables and hundreds of horses and carriages. This Main Street view captures the era after the arrival of electricity, the telegraph, and telephones but before the advent of streetlights and cars. Note the baby strollers in the foreground on the right.

MAIN STREET LOOKING NORTH, C. 1940. As a retail and entertainment destination, downtown Port Henry reached a new peak in the 1940s, with dozens of shops, cafes, bars, and the Essex movie theater. This photograph, taken from almost the same location as the 1905-era view above, shows the removal of overhead power lines and the advent of the angled car parking that still exists today. Maturing elm trees help to frame the entry view.

"THE SQUARE" IN PORT HENRY, 1907 POSTCARD. Likely taken just before the advent of the automobile, this view shows the monumental architecture of its retail and cultural buildings. A grocery and provisions store occupied the ground floor of the Lewald Opera House. All along Main Street, colorful awnings helped block strong sunlight on the stores. This original bandstand sits at the center of everything.

LEWALD OPERA HOUSE AFTER FIRE, 1910. Built at a cost of $30,000, the Lewald Opera House was the site of many musicals and concerts by renowned performers. It was destroyed by fire on December 12, 1910. The following year, the Foote Block, home to shops and apartments, was built on this highly visible site.

WESTON BROS. MEATS & GROCERIES, C. 1900. Located near the current Celotti's Wine and Spirits, Weston Bros. burned in the Lewald Opera House fire in 1910. Here, family and friends of the Westons came together to pose for this photograph. The boy on the left seems to be wearing a sailor's outfit.

FOOTE BLOCK, 1912 POSTCARD. Probably taken just after the new Foote Block was completed, this photograph shows the new storefronts for the Weston Market and N. Berman Wholesale Grocer next door. With green-inset terra-cotta tiles, red Spanish tile cornices, and elegant metal store window canopies, the Foote Block represented the newly fashionable Craftsman style of design and boasted handmade details such as carved wooden eave brackets and beautiful brickwork.

46

BROAD STREET LOOKING WEST, C. 1930. The elegant masonry bandstand, with its trees and column lights, created a one-of-a-kind focus for downtown. Note the information sign near the stairs, giving directions and distances to Mineville, Crown Point, and Ticonderoga. Car travel was slower and more romantic then, but it was surely much more dangerous as well, with narrow roads, diagonal street parking, and no seat belts.

MAIN STREET LOOKING NORTH, C. 1930. By the end of the Roaring Twenties, downtown Port Henry was filled with electric store signs, most of which jutted out from the storefronts. Angled parking lined both sides of the streets, and the elm trees planted in the 1880s and 1890s were coming into maturity. This view looks much the same today, although, sadly, the trees are gone.

CHAMPLAINETTE LIME, C. 1910 BOTTLE LABEL. Located on Convent Hill, Lake Champlain Bottling Works used the "pure Adirondack mountain water" from area springs and streams to create a wide variety of beverages. Before the advent of truck delivery, many small towns had their own bottling works and breweries to serve close-by communities. Today, Lake Champlain bottles with labels such as this one are highly collectible.

NEW LEE HOUSE, 1926. The Lee House hotel opened in 1877 and was modernized in the early 1900s. This 1920s photograph shows the hotel's vertical electric-bulb sign, elegant porch, and colorful awnings. Many noted visitors and silent film stars working at Arctic City Studios stayed at the Lee House during this time. Today, the Lee House is listed in the National Register of Historic Places and serves as senior housing.

CEDAR POINT HOUSE BAR. In the late 19th century, there were many lodges and boarding houses in Moriah that catered to business travelers and early tourists who came for hunting and fishing. With a pressed-tin ceiling and a beautiful wooden bar and backdrop, the Cedar Point House was an attractive place to meet for a drink. Cedar Point House, which is now privately owned, is just south of downtown Port Henry on Route 9N, offered lodging and dining. Owner Patrick Callaghan, with the suit on, is pictured here with the bartenders.

THE LIGHT THAT SERVES ME SHINES FOR ALL.

W. H. BIGALOW,

Photographer,

PORT HENRY,   N. Y.

W.H. BIGALOW, PHOTOGRAPHER. From the late 1800s well into the 1920s, W.H. Bigalow photographed most of the important people and events in Port Henry and Moriah. Bigalow's business card from around 1900 was printed on thick paper stock with his own portrait on the back. Several of his photographs are included in this book, including photographs of Port Henry's railroad station.

PORTRAIT OF CHURCH LADIES BY W.H. BIGALOW, C. 1900. This playful large-format photograph is typical of W.H. Bigalow's professional work. Here, he shows five young women of the Victorian era linking arms on the south lawn of the First Presbyterian Church. Perhaps they are bridesmaids or members of a church club. They all wear long black gloves and hats that complement their white dresses and skirts, which they gracefully lift for a flowing effect. (Courtesy of the Sherman Free Library.)

50

BANDSTAND AND WATER TROUGH, PORT HENRY, 1918. Completed in 1906, Port Henry's second bandstand expressed the ideals of the City Beautiful Movement that came to life with the popularity of the Chicago World's Fair in 1893. A horse-watering trough, lion-head fountain, and bandstand illuminated by electric globes, this structure was one of the most elegant and beautiful street features of any town in New York. Taken a few years after completion, this professional photograph from Witherbee, Sherman & Company shows the symmetry of the bandstand and fountain at the center of Broad and Main Streets. During the rush to modernize in the 1950s, and with a likely exaggerated fear of water contamination, the bandstand was demolished in 1953. Many people still regret its loss today. However, a new version of the fountain has recently returned. In 2011, local master stonemason Pat Salerno, with the help of citizen volunteers, built a new, smaller fountain on this site with a lion's head spouting water, recalling the original.

HENRY'S GARAGE AT 25. When the new four-story garage was still relatively new, the Henry family celebrated their 25th anniversary of being in business as a livery and car operation dating back to horse-and-buggy days. This is likely a parade float on an early flatbed truck, with a car set on its cargo hold advertising the Henry name. (Courtesy of the Deborah Henry collection.)

SUPER IGA MARKET, C. 1950. Just up Broad Street from downtown Port Henry, the IGA was one of Moriah's largest supermarkets for decades. The store occupied the main floor of a three-story apartment building that was made of blocks of mine tailings. Today, the former store bays are apartments.

HENRY'S GARAGE DEALERSHIP, 1948. Built by C.W. Henry and his sons Ray, Earl, and Harold in 1910, Henry's Garage still stands on Church Street as the home of the Port Henry Fire Department, which moved in after the Henry's Chrysler dealership closed in 1969. The four-story Henry's building is one of the few garages in the country built during the transition from horses to cars and designed to serve both. The Henrys originally ran a livery stable on the site. The upper floors housed cars and car repairs. Most remarkable of all, Henry's Garage was built of mining tailings mixed with concrete and designed by young Earl Henry as a modern service garage. He conceived it for his senior engineering thesis at Rensselaer Polytechnic Institute (RPI), the renowned engineering school in Troy. Today, the fire department stores and maintains its equipment on the main level. (Courtesy of the Anna Beebe collection.)

MARTIN'S REXALL DRUGS, 1948. Many of Port Henry's downtown buildings express "layers of time" through changes in architectural fashion. This mid-1800s brick residence is the home to today's Moriah Pharmacy, a mainstay in downtown Port Henry. After World War II, Martin's Rexall, the prior business, modernized their storefront with large, open display windows and a neon sign set into a sleek enamel facade. This modern update happened about a century after the Federal-style residence was built. Yet, there are other styles here too, like the later Greek Revival–style return cornices and the Italianate window hoods on the second stories. Like many North Country buildings, the layering of styles reflects generations of additions, renovations, and new technologies. The pharmacy is one of the oldest buildings in downtown Port Henry, likely dating from the Federal era of design in the 1840s. (Courtesy of the Anna Beebe collection.)

PORT HENRY'S DINER. One of the oldest and most intact Ward & Dickinson Co. diners in the country still operates in Port Henry and is well known by diner buffs. Company founder Charles A. Ward submitted the design to the patent office in 1927. It opened first in Glens Falls and then moved to its Port Henry location in 1933. The surviving wheels are extremely rare for a diner of this era. The diner, originally named Miss Port Henry, is now called Foote's Port Henry Diner, and the old dining car still operates today with its original cream and green exterior restored. Many of the interior features, including the stools and wooden shelving, still survive. In the winter, beautiful sunlight streams in through the diner's tall windows to illuminate the marble counter tops. (Photograph by Janet Beebe Denney.)

OFFICER BURZEE, 1967. After the grand second bandstand was removed in the 1950s, the village built a small circular garden. Here, Kenneth Burzee, Port Henry's fire police officer, stands by to direct traffic and probably a parade. In the background, the Essex Theater is still in operation, and citizens and flags line the sidewalks.

GROVER H. BAXTER AND SCHOOLCHILDREN, 1932. A much-beloved Port Henry citizen, Grover Baxter served as mayor, fire chief, the local taxi driver, and a chauffeur. Here, he wears his chauffeur's cap and suit as he drives the local school bus on Edgemont Road. The young boy hanging out of the front door is Freeman Beebe, whose family has farmed on the road for generations. (Courtesy of the Dorothy Baxter Wilber collection.)

Five

MORIAH'S VILLAGES AND THE COMPANY TOWNS OF MINEVILLE AND WITHERBEE

WITHERBEE, C. 1900. On the left side of this panoramic view, Witherbee, Sherman & Company separators process ore for transfer on the Lake Champlain & Moriah Railway down to Port Henry. To the lower right, a loaded train of ore cars heads east. Along the top of the photograph, newly built multiple-unit and single-family homes for miners are punctuated with street trees. Above everything, Witherbee's St. Michael's Catholic Church and parsonage overlooks life and work.

MORIAH CENTER, C. 1910. Driving down the hill from Moriah Corners, travelers used to see this view of Moriah Center. To the right is a landmark two-story bandstand. On the left is Louis Deyo's store, next to Sprague's (later Bolles') Store. Straight ahead is the Ryan Hennessy Block, which still stands today.

MORIAH CENTER CONCERT BAND, 1911 POSTCARD. Before radio and records, almost every small town had a concert band. Many of the villages in Moriah had a bandstand prominently located at the center of town. With vistas of Lake Champlain, Moriah Center retains much of its historical charm today. In 1911, its band included several generations. (Courtesy of the Anna Beebe collection.)

HOTEL SHERMAN, C. 1900 POSTCARD. This early postcard shows the now lost Hotel Sherman in the village of Moriah. With broad porches on the front and sides, the Sherman set out wooden armchairs and rockers so that guests could take advantage of cool summer breezes. Built entirely of wood, the hotel's Greek Revival architecture, popular through much of New York in the mid-1800s, included evenly spaced columns and a roof shape reminiscent of an ancient temple.

FLIER FOR MARTIN CONDON'S STORE, C. 1880. Each of Moriah's villages had a variety of grocery stores that sold flour, salt, sugar, and other staples for the pantry. They also sold provisions like soap, sewing needles, pots and pans, and other dry goods. This card from Martin Condon's store in Mineville is part of a promotion for Lautz Bros. & Co. Marseilles White Soap. When customers saved up enough wrappers, they could send them in for prizes. (Courtesy of the Anna Beebe collection.)

WITHERBEE, SHERMAN & COMPANY HEADQUARTERS, MINEVILLE. This early-1900s postcard shows the massive staircase that connected Witherbee Memorial Hall, the Lake Champlain & Moriah Railroad, and the core of Mineville to the Witherbee, Sherman & Company offices. Note the early tree plantings and the large concrete and stone retaining wall against the steep grade.

E.P. CLONAN RESIDENCE. A superintendent at Witherbee, Sherman & Company, E.P. Clonan lived in this elegant home on Fisher Hill Road in Mineville. It features a slate roof and picturesque style. Note the large wraparound porch, ideal for relaxing on long summer evenings. More recently, the house was Gloria's Restaurant, which attracted customers from Vermont and the local area.

60

CONCRETE HIGH SCHOOL IN MINEVILLE, 1918. Witherbee, Sherman & Company built many public facilities for its employees, including this concrete high school that operated until it was consolidated into the Moriah Central School District in 1967. Located near Memorial Hall and the Mineville headquarters of Witherbee, Sherman & Company, the school was a center of the community for many decades.

HOSPITAL IN MINEVILLE. Witherbee, Sherman & Company was very paternalistic towards its employees and their families. By subsidizing their housing, schools, community centers, and health care, the company sought to maintain a productive workforce. Located next to its Mineville headquarters, this hospital still stands as a reminder of company life.

De Lalla's Rexall Drug in Mineville, 1952. Built in 1909 of molded block made with mine tailings and concrete, this storefront remains a Mineville landmark on the corner of Main and Maple Streets. An elegant balustrade adorns the balcony porch, extending from the upstairs apartment where the shop owners once lived. On the main floor, high ceilings and diamond-grid transom windows bring sunlight deep into the store.

Scozzafava's Store in Mineville, c. 1940. For many years, area children loved the ice cream served in the soda fountain at Scozzafava's. Here, Thomas Scozzafava stands proudly outside his business. Note the signs for ice cream and Salada Tea in the background.

MINEVILLE HIGH SCHOOL GIRLS' BASKETBALL TEAM, 1937–1938. The high school was a vital source of identity and pride for Mineville—and so were its sports teams. This well-funded school offered a variety of sports and was perhaps ahead of its time in offering sports such as basketball for female students. In this group shot, probably taken at the end of the season, the girls smile happily for the camera. They had a very successful season that year, winning all six of their games. Their coach, Adele Jurek, stands on the right. (Courtesy of the Peggy Porter collection.)

PARK STREET IN MINEVILLE, C. 1940. Witherbee, Sherman & Company built neighborhoods of wood-frame single-family houses for managers and their families. In Mineville, this row of Craftsman- and Dutch Colonial–style houses looks much the same today. They were built in the 1920s and 1930s with porches, indoor plumbing, and modern kitchens for the time. The houses are now privately owned.

DOUBLE HOUSE FOR CLERKS, 1918. Like many mining towns, Witherbee and Mineville were stratified according to rank and role within the company. Small apartments were rented to single miners, whereas white-collar employees such as clerks were allotted larger double houses, like this one in Mineville. The use of concrete tailings block and the gambrel-shaped roofs unified everything. (Courtesy of the Sherman Free Library.)

ELM STREET IN WITHERBEE, 1918. Designed by engineers from Witherbee, Sherman & Company, Mineville's worker housing was built in response to concerns over worker safety and fires after the disastrous Triangle Shirt Company fire in New York City. Still lived in today, Mineville's single and multiunit homes were built of block that mixed concrete and mine tailings. With gambrel -shaped roofs, each of these new houses for young families on "Bridal Row" proudly boasts a fenced front yard and newly planted elm trees.

FOUR-FAMILY HOUSE, 1918. In addition to single, double, and triple houses, Witherbee, Sherman & Company also built four-family tenements, possible for occupation by single miners. They were constructed of mine tailings mixed with concrete. Note the line of block that divides the first and second floors. Like all of the miner houses, these homes originally did not have indoor plumbing. (Courtesy of the Sherman Free Library.)

MINEVILLE HIGH SCHOOL TRACK TEAM, C. 1930. This team portrait says much about life and education in Mineville in the 1920s and 1930s. This was an era of great prosperity for the community, even as Witherbee, Sherman & Company, challenged by emerging competition and high debts, struggled to remain profitable. Decades of company and community investments in schools, hospitals, housing, and tree planting were paying off in Mineville, with a vibrant commercial community with many activities for young people. As seen here, the young people were generally fit from summer work, lots of walking to get around, and a diet without today's processed food.

Taken in front of Mineville's high school, this photograph shows a district school bus—quite an investment at the time—on the left and the Witherbee, Sherman & Company office building on top of the hill to the right. In the top left corner is the clubhouse, where visiting officials and businesspeople could stay. In the foreground, the team proudly displays a trophy. Standing on the left and right of the second row are two teacher/coaches with their fairly long hair combed back, which must have been the style then. (Courtesy of the Peggy Porter collection.)

St. Peter and Paul's Church Today. Still operating as a parish in Mineville, St. Peter and Paul's Church served the many Polish and Italian families who lived in the village. Today, the church holds an active worship program and is home to a fine pipe organ and stained glass. It is now called All Saints Church.

MINEVILLE HIGH SCHOOL
ALMA MATER

Far up in the Adirondacks, with their sights so fair
Stands our noble Alma Mater, with her chances rare.
Lift the chorus, speed it onward, with your might
    and will!

Hail to thee our Alma Mater, hail, all hail Mineville!
In the midst of Old Man Winter, when the snow
    drifts deep;

In the glory of the summer, we her honor keep.
In the writing of her history, pages we will fill,
This refrain oft times repeated, hail, all hail Mine-
ville.

Compliments of

Champlain Agency Corp.

Mineville, New York

"Bud" and Marie Thompson, Agents

MINEVILLE HIGH SCHOOL

33rd Annual

Alumni Banquet

V. F. W. HOME

Mineville, New York

★

Saturday, June 26, 1971

Mineville High School Song and Reunion Guide, 1971. Before the creation of the Moriah Central School District in 1967, the village of Mineville had its own high school, which also served Witherbee. Located next to Memorial Hall (today's VFW), the high school was at the heart of the mining operations. (Courtesy of the Anna Beebe collection.)

THE "POLISH" CHURCH IN
WITHERBEE, C. 1920. Located on
the old Plank Road, Mineville's
Catholic church was organized
in 1872, and this building was
constructed in 1875. The church
is no longer operating, and this
landmark building set high over
Witherbee is now a privately
owned. The church served -
immigrant miners for decades,
who were, as the nickname
implies, largely Polish.

CENTRAL RESTAURANT IN WITHERBEE, 1954. Not surprisingly, with the large population of
Italian American families drawn to mining, Witherbee boasted an Italian restaurant. In this
winter scene, note the modern-style neon sign jutting out over the sidewalk. Central Restaurant
was built by Joseph and Alphorsina Neggia in the 1930s as a wooden addition to the front of one
of the Witherbee, Sherman & Company tailings-block houses.

THREE NEW FORDS, C. 1940. For many years, the Pepper family ran a general store and post office in the hamlet of Moriah. This photograph celebrates the day that Walt Pepper and each of his two sons bought new Fords from the Belden dealership in Port Henry. Standing proudly in front of the Pepper's store, Walt (center) shakes hands with Charlie Belden. On the left, Stanley Pepper stands with his new Ford alongside the family dog, Sandy. To the right, Bob Pepper and his new Ford fill out the trio. (Courtesy of the Peggy Porter collection.)

INDUSTRIAL RUIN. This photograph shows one of the many Republic Steel ore separators standing abandoned with its windows and railroad track still intact. Most of these old buildings would still be standing if not for concerns over injury and liability lawsuits. The dangers of old shafts and massive, multilevel empty buildings led Republic Steel to sell such facilities or demolish them.

EQUIPMENT SHED. Taken at the same time as the previous photograph of the abandoned ore separator, this equipment shed built of tailings block stands next to a formal rail line and an ore loader. Like much of the Republic Steel infrastructure, this utilitarian building is now demolished. Such old buildings, if they survive, could one day find a new use as residences, small factories, or studios. Patrick Farrel, a former Republic Steel employee, knew these industrial settings and their sounds. In his compelling book about Moriah's mining history, *Through the Light Hole*, he wrote, "The town is quiet now. There is a new generation of adults who have never heard the whine of the winding hoist ropes; the rumble of skips bringing ore to the surface; the thumping sound of the jaw crusher and ore striking the sides of metal storage bins." He goes on to describe the now-vanished "wailful" sound of the train whistles bringing ore down from the mines to the lake. "Only photographs remain of the hundred-foot-high headframes outlined against the sky," he writes.

GROVER HILLS TODAY. In 1942, the Federal Public Housing Authority built 430 housing units spread over two new neighborhoods for mining war workers. Moricette Heights, named for Edward J. Moricette, the first Mineville serviceman to die in World War II, was later demolished. Grover Hills was named for John Oscar Grover, the first Moriah soldier to die in the war. Many of the homes from Grover Hills survive and are independently owned today. (Photograph by Janet Beebe Denney.)

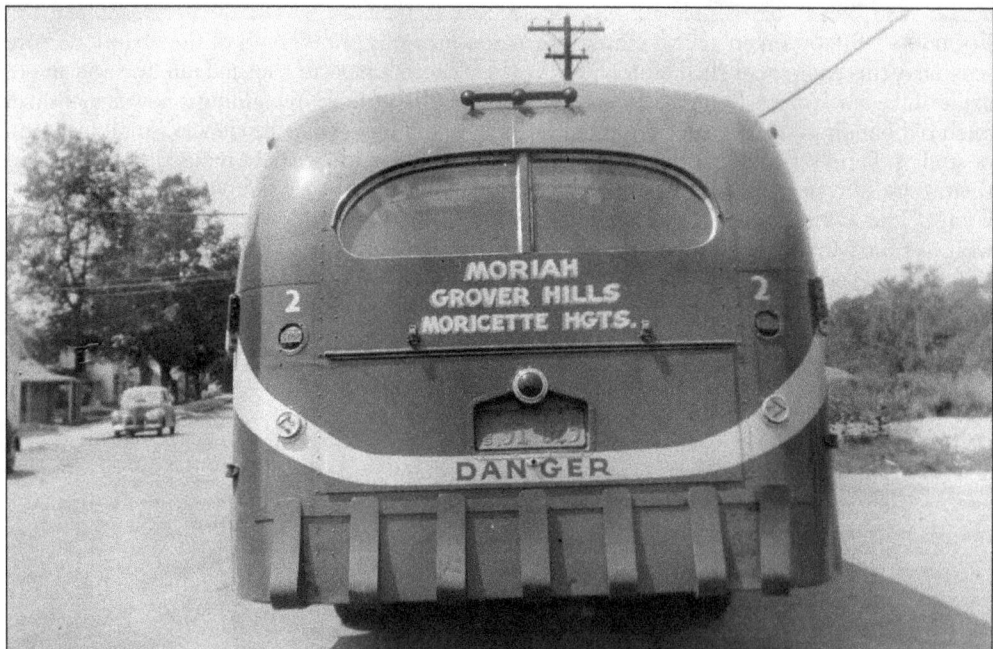

PUBLIC BUS DURING WARTIME. This photograph shows the rear of a public bus that was likely used to bring workers from Moriah and the purpose-built wartime neighborhoods of Grover Hills and Moricette Heights to jobs in Mineville and other processing mills. Given gas rationing and the cost of cars, it is unlikely that many of the newly arrived war workers drove themselves. (Courtesy of the Anna Beebe collection.)

Six

PORT HENRY'S
NEIGHBORHOODS AND HOMES

LEDGESIDE, C. 1910. Around 1880, Frank S. Witherbee built a majestic Second Empire–style mansion known as Ledgeside. With a formal lawn and garden facing Main Street and views over Lake Champlain and Crown Point, Ledgeside was one of the grandest houses in the region. Witherbee's home and grounds are now owned by Mountain Lake Services, and the striking lakeside lawn next to St. Patrick's Church is open to the public.

GARDEN AT LEDGESIDE, C. 1890. Enclosed by a wrought-iron fence along Main Street and bounded by trees, Ledgeside was a formal mansion that would have been at home in many larger cities. Lined with rose bushes, this rolled-clay path greeted visitors as they arrived from Main Street. Note the well-manicured grass panels on either side of the path and the ivy covering much of the house. Ledgeside's lawn facing the lake was less formal, with grass that swept off to the crest of the bluff. It is rumored that Witherbee had many collections, including an Egyptian mummy. In the summer, palms and other tropical plants from Ledgeside's conservatory were brought outside and set along the paths. Facing Main Street, a large portico and two-story porch greeted visitors arriving by carriage. At the top of the center cupola, an American flag proudly flew.

CREW AT LEDGESIDE, C. 1880. It took many craftspeople to build Ledgeside, and many more to keep it running as a full-service mansion through the years. In this well-composed photograph of workers sitting on the porch overlooking Lake Champlain, there are many kinds of outfits. Perhaps the two men sitting on the steps to the lower left are masons. The man wearing a hat and apron near the center appears to be holding a carpenter's square. There are many trades represented here. It is likely that this photograph was taken just as the house was nearing completion around 1880, as the grass and paintwork all appear quite new and the latticework under the porch seems perfect. This was a time when many professions and building trades adopted their own particular type of work clothes. Posing together, these men at Ledgeside make quite a fashion statement. It was an era of craftsmanship and detailed ornament—and everyone wore hats.

LEDGETOP, 1902 PANORAMIC PHOTOGRAPH. Set high on Port Henry's hillside and surrounded by tall pines, Silas Witherbee's son, Walter C. Witherbee, constructed one of the finest shingle-style residences in the Adirondacks. Built in the Richardsonian Romanesque style, this 12,500-square-foot mansion has remarkable details, including 1,200 square feet of covered porches and cupolas with panoramic views. There were also greenhouses and carriage barns, which are in the background. In early decades, Ledgetop was a working farm with vegetable gardens and even a chicken coop, which survives at the back entry to the kitchen wing. To the right, behind the house, note the roofs and cupolas of neighboring houses and outbuildings. For its time, Ledgetop was very modern,

with fairly simple large windows and shingled siding that anticipates the soon-to-be-popular shingle style. This panoramic photograph looking north in winter shows wheel ruts left in the snow from horses pulling carriages along the looping entry drive. Young spruce and other ornamental trees are beginning to rise over the fine stone gates and perimeter wall that stretches north all the way to the rear of the photograph. Ledgetop, which is currently undergoing rehabilitation, remains one of the finest Richardsonian shingle-style mansions in all of New York. (Courtesy of the Sherman Free Library.)

SWIMMING POOL AT LEDGETOP, C. 1920. On the northwest corner of Ledgetop lies a fairly intact former concrete swimming pool that the Witherbees and their guests enjoyed in the early and mid-1900s. At one time, probably in the 1920s, the pool was surrounded with beautiful spruce trees and beds of old-fashioned perennial flowers. Apparently, the pool was originally part of a foundation for a building that is long gone. Today, a century-old ginkgo tree visible from Broad Street stands tall. No doubt, this ginkgo, an ancient species native to China, was planted as part of a larger landscape plan around 1900. It is probably one of the oldest ginkgo trees in all of the North Country. Ledgetop's thick stone retaining walls along Broad Street and an elegant stone stairway connecting the street to a long-lost hillside path are all slated for eventual landscape restoration.

GEO. C. FOOTE'S RES., PORT HENRY, N.Y. NO. 25.

W.J. FOOTE RESIDENCE, C. 1910. This photograph shows the porches, awnings, and gambrel roof of the W.J. Foote residence, set on a commanding hillside just north of Port Henry. Foote made his fortune as an early investor in mining. He later invested in real estate, building the Foote Block. Today, his large residence is owned by Mountain Lake Services.

Port Henry NY From Res: H on W.J. Foote

VIEW FROM FOOTE RESIDENCE, 1912 POSTCARD. Overlooking Lake Champlain and Port Henry, the Foote estate boasted some of the most beautiful gardens and views in Port Henry, including this vista of downtown with a cast-iron fountain in the foreground. In the early 1900s, the Lake Champlain Fish & Game Club had a rifle and skeet range on what was called Foote's meadow.

ENTRY TO THE DALLIBA RESIDENCE, C. 1900. Built in the 1820s, the Maj. James Dalliba residence was one of the first large homes in Port Henry. This view looks through its handcrafted stone gates to the entry drive. Designed for carriages, the drive looped downhill from this entry off of today's Route 9N, past the main house and the servants' quarters just to the south, and then back down to the road. The stone wall and the servants' quarters still stand.

VIEW OF PORT HENRY FROM CONVENT HILL, C. 1915 POSTCARD. Looking southward towards St. Patrick's Church and downtown Port Henry, this view remains much the same today. For 150 years, Port Henry has always been a village nestled along a hill, and its dense clusters of buildings and winding Main Street entry from the north still lend it a distinctive character among Lake Champlain towns.

GEORGE R. SHERMAN HOME, C. 1900. Built by George Riley Sherman, the cofounder of Witherbee, Sherman & Company, this mid-19th-century mansion on Port Henry's Main Street looks much the same today. It is now a local landmark as the Harland Funeral Home. The lawns and house are carefully maintained, and old iron urns still hold flowers near the front entry.

THE KING'S INN, 1952. Built by a member of the Witherbee family in the early 1900s, this hilltop mansion is known today as the King's Inn. As a social center for Moriah, the King's Inn is popular for its tavern, its restaurant, and the beautiful lodgings upstairs in the elegant bedrooms. Today, the shingle siding and stone facade remains, although the porch has been enclosed as a dining area.

GARDEN AT THE DALLIBA/FOOTE RESIDENCE, C. 1930. In the 1820s, Maj. James Dalliba became one of the first investors to develop the mines in the Port Henry area. In 1824, he constructed a large frame house on the west side of Highway 9N on the northern edge of the village. The old house's foundations and walls still remain. In the rear of the house, the Footes developed remarkable formal gardens and paths. Seen here is the perennial garden and linear path leading around a cast-iron fountain and back into the hillside. Remarkably, remnants of this path and the fountain base still remain.

Posing in the Garden, c. 1930. The Footes, who took over the Dalliba gardens, must have been a playful family because they liked to pose in costumes in their garden. Here, two women and a boy with long blond hair stand before a bower covered with clematis. The boy's hat and tunic seem Dutch or French. Perhaps they were dressed up to put on a play or concert. In the foreground, a bed of iris may have just finished blooming. Today, the Greek Revival double house built for the Dallibas' servants is still occupied next door. The entire site is bounded by an original stone wall with an iron gate. Trees have grown up to obscure the views of Lake Champlain that existed in the 1800s.

NEW SPRING STREET RESIDENCE, C. 1895. Set on the top of the hill overlooking Lake Champlain, this new house with its Eastlake-style details in the gable ends and brackets must have been the height of fashion for the time. Though relatively small, the house is designed for optimal sunlight and cross-ventilation. Note the wooden walk extending outward to the street.

SPRING STREET LOOKING SOUTH, C. 1915 POSTCARD. A century ago, Spring Street was one of the most beautiful areas of Port Henry, and it still is today. With an elevated location and views into Vermont, Spring Street was the home for many leaders of Port Henry's prosperous businesses and the mining industry. Taken before the roadway was paved, this view shows two of the impressive shingle and Queen Anne houses that still stand at the top of Spring Street today.

HELIUS SISTERS, 1903. Dressed in their best winter finery, Susie (left) and Jennie Helius pose on Spring Street to have their photograph taken by Sadie MacDonald, a neighbor or friend. With its large trees and broad views, Spring Street looks much the same today.

REV. LEWIS FRANCIS RESIDENCE, C. 1900. This postcard shows the view from the home of Rev. Lewis Francis at the edge of the village of Port Henry. The Adirondack foothills in the background and the steep slopes and valleys look much the same today; although, like much of the village, these hillsides are no longer grazed or burned and have thus been covered with trees.

85

FOOTE GAZEBO. Located high over the lake, the Foote residence had a little bit of everything: cast-iron fountains, statues, gardens, and even a gazebo. This dramatic postcard shows the rock face along the lakeshore and the tunnel cut through it for passing trains. Notice the sloped "witch's hat" roof and the surrounding terrace and railing. The small structure nestles into the hilltop on a base of latticework.

VIEW NEAR WITHERBEE, SHERMAN & COMPANY OFFICES, C. 1910. This beautiful view, looking east towards Lake Champlain, shows Park Place much as it looks today. A century ago, there were more buildings along the street. What remains today is the broad vista of the lake, the town hall (which is in the former Witherbee, Sherman & Company offices), and a new gazebo and bandstand in the park seen here. The white house to the left is now the town courthouse.

Seven

ARTS AND RECREATION

MOTORING ALONG ROUTE 9N, c. 1925 POSTCARD. In the early years of cars, when motoring was a novel and popular form of recreation, Route 9N was a well-traveled road. It was one of the most beautiful and dramatic routes along Lake Champlain. This postcard captures a vista of Port Henry and its lakefront, which looks much the same today when drivers travel through the rock-cuts just south of the village.

TRAVELING CAROUSEL, C. 1890. Covered with a circus tent, this carousel came to Mineville every summer for many years in the late 1800s. To the right, a man operates the steam engine that made the horses and the merry-go-round turn. Moving from town to town, the setup of the carousel and tent must have been quite a job.

PORT HENRY COUNTRY CLUB AND CLUB HOUSE, C. 1920. Golf has always been a very popular sport in the summer. Mrs. Frank Witherbee developed the Port Henry Country Club in 1900. It is one of the oldest nine-hole courses in the United States that is open to the public. The course winds through a small valley with a brook on the lower holes.

SHERMAN RACETRACK SCORECARD, 1902. Located on Forge Hollow Road, George D. Sherman built a horse-racing track that operated for many years. Sherman owned a large string of trotters and pacers that were trained here for the Grand Circuit Races. This wonderful piece of paper ephemera is a small stapled booklet that race-goers could buy for 10¢ to keep track of the horses and their results. At the time of this publication, September 1902, the track was known as the Sherman Trotting Park. George D. Sherman is remembered as the somewhat profligate son of George Riley Sherman, the cofounder of Witherbee, Sherman & Company. As for his interest in horse racing, it is believed that he had another, more remote track near Witherbee. Some stories claim that, on occasion, he would invite many of his male friends to Port Henry and hire a group of female performers from a Folies Bergère–type troupe to delight his guests by running scantily clad around the track—a somewhat unusual form of recreation. (Courtesy of the Peggy Porter collection.)

89

PORT HENRY BASEBALL TEAM, C. 1905 POSTCARD. Port Henry has a long tradition of excellence in baseball, and many of the surrounding villages, including Mineville and Moriah Center, had their own teams. In this view, likely taken just before the advent of the motorcar, Port Henry's well-dressed baseball team poses. The dapper man at the rear center in a necktie and hat is likely their coach. (Courtesy of the Anna Beebe collection.)

BASEBALL GAME IN PORT HENRY, 1908 POSTCARD. A sizable crowd attends a baseball game at a local field. Motorcars were just beginning to be used in 1908, and some were driven to this game, along with horse-drawn buggies. (Courtesy of the Sherman Free Library.)

COUNTRY SCHOOL PORTRAIT, 1898. This beautiful photograph shows students from the Sprague District School No. 12 and their teacher, Nell Shaw, posing on a rocky hillside. As was the case in many one-room country schools, these children are of many different ages. Shaw sits proudly in the top right. This portrait was taken in Shaw's pasture, near North Hudson Road in Moriah. Children often seem very serious in old photographs such as this one, but modern viewers forget that they had to sit still for several seconds as the glass plate in the camera exposed. (Courtesy of the Peggy Porter collection.)

LEWALD OPERA HOUSE

Port Henry, N. Y.,

DECEMBER 4, '82.

PROGRAMME

1. PIANO SOLO— - - - - - Selected.
    MR. JOSEPH HARRISON.

2. SONG—"I Love my Love," - - - Mackey.
    MISS ANNIE E. BEERE.

3. VIOLONCELLO SOLO—"Danse Hollandaise," - Dunkler.
    MR. LOUIS BLUMENBERG.

4. ARIA—"Qui La Voce," (Puritani,) - - Bellini.
    MLLE. MARIE LITTA.

5. ARIA—"La Forza del Destino," - - - Verdi.
    SIG. E. BALDANZA.

   ARIA—"Magic Flute," - - - - Mozart.
    MR. JULIUS BEREGHY.

7. DUET—"Trovatore." - - - - Verdi.
    MLLE. MARIE LITTA and SIG. ERNESTO BALDANZA.

8. "BALLET MUSIC," - - - - Rubenstein.
    MR. JOSEPH HARRISON.

9. SONG—"Sweethearts," - - - Sullivan.
    MISS ANNIE E. BEERE.

10. VIOLONCELLO SOLO— {(a). Romanza, - Sivori.
    {(b). Spinning Wheel, - Davidoff.

11. ARIA— - - - - - Selected.
    MLLE MARIA LITTA.

12. QUARTETTE—"Rigoletto," - - - Verdi.
    MLLE. MARIE LITTA. MISS ANNIE E. BEERE.
    SIG. ERNESTO BALDANZA. JULIUS BEREGHY.

CONCERT PROGRAM FOR LEWALD OPERA HOUSE, DECEMBER 4, 1882. Port Henry was a center for culture and performance, especially during the winter seasons. Built and supported through donations, the Lewald Opera House was a center for music, lectures, and dramatic performances. The program for December 4, 1882, included a mix of piano, popular songs, "ballet music," and opera. Several once-famous performers appeared at the Lewald Opera House. Port Henry, with its many schools and talented citizens, also contributed performers. (Courtesy of the Sherman Free Library.)

LEWALD OPERA HOUSE, 1906. By the end of the 1800s, downtown Port Henry was one of the most "cultured" destinations on Lake Champlain. This postcard, looking east down Broad Street, shows the newly constructed concrete bandstand, the Second Empire–style Lewald Opera House to the left, and the Van Ornam & Murdock Block, which still stands today.

1880

"MANY RARE CURIOSITIES," 1880 ADVERTISEMENT. A mummy's hand, ancient coins, and Indian relics were all part of the "valuable curiosities" in this traveling museum that came to Port Henry in 1880. Harking back to the "cabinets of curiosities" that were the first museums of the Renaissance, Port Henry's show included anthropological artifacts from distant lands, relics from the classical world of Greece and Rome, and oddities linking the natural and the cultural such as a "petrified hat." Residents could visit many times, always finding something new. Season tickets cost 75¢. (Courtesy of the Sherman Free Library.)

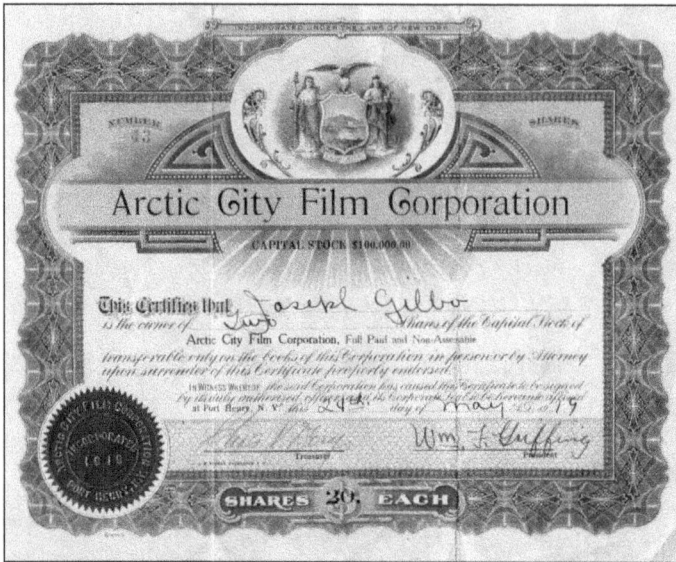

STOCK CERTIFICATE, ARCTIC CITY FILM CORPORATION, 1919. Issued to Port Henry resident Joseph Gilbo on May 24, 1919, this engraved stock certificate boasts that the Arctic City Film Corporation was capitalized at $100,000. Gilbo purchased two shares at $20 each. Today, Moriah residents remember hearing Arctic City stories from their grandparents, some of whom served as extras in the many productions from 1915 to 1926.

ARCTIC CITY IN THE MOONLIGHT, C. 1920 PROMOTIONAL IMAGE. Founded in Port Henry in 1915 by colorful dogsled racer William F. Cooper, better known as "Caribou Bill," the Arctic City movie studio became an instant Western frontier town, complete with mountain backdrops and abundant snow for winter filming. Caribou Bill also kept dogsled teams on-site for use in filming. Located near today's Moriah Central School, Arctic City thrived from 1916 into the mid-1920s. Numerous production companies, including Vitagraph and the Metro Feature Company, rented the "studio" for productions. In the winter of 1920, three movie companies—the Charles Miller Production Co., the William Fox Film Co., and Goldwyn—were each making films at Arctic City.

MOVIE STARS AT ARCTIC CITY, 1920. *The Law of Yukon*, a Klondike gold rush tale, was one of the most expensive silent films ever shot in the Adirondacks. Seen in this shot taken during filming are, from left to right, star Pearl White and local actors Wally Carr and Esther Johnson Donahue. Famous stars like White often stayed at the elegant Lee House in downtown Port Henry.

ARCTIC HOTEL AT ARCTIC CITY, 1916. The Arctic City Film Corporation built mountain town sets for winter shooting. There were entire shells of buildings complete with signs and porches, like the Arctic Hotel, seen here.

PORT HENRY HIGH SCHOOL BASKETBALL TEAM, 1914. The 1913–1914 season for Port Henry's basketball team must have been a good one, because the team is posing here in a formal studio setting with two trophies.

TOM TYLER AS CAPTAIN MARVEL, C. 1945. Besides its silent film history, Moriah is also home to a few movie stars, including Tom Tyler who started out as an actor in Westerns before moving on to superhero themes. He is seen here in his role as Captain Marvel in a studio shot.

C. ELEANOR HALL, C. 1940. Most of the images in this book are available today because Eleanor Hall (1901–1999) had the foresight to save them many years ago. As Moriah's town historian for 46 years, from 1945 to 1991, she gathered hundreds of photographs, letters, pamphlets, and books that would later form the core collection of the Moriah Historical Society. Hall was a graduate of Port Henry High School, attended Mount Holyoke College, and obtained a degree in library science from Simmons College. Her interest in history led to a collaboration with Dr. Charles W. Warner in 1931 to publish *The History of the Port Henry, N.Y.*, a book that informed much of the writing in this volume. Hall was also a great lover of maps; in 1934, she published a pictorial map called "A Romance Map of the Northern Gateway" that featured historical events in northeastern New York and northwestern Vermont. She also wrote numerous articles on Lake Champlain history and the culture of ice fishing.

JOHNNY PODRES SIGN ON ROUTE 9N. Johnny Podres was born in 1932 and grew up in Witherbee, where he learned to play baseball. He was a left-handed pitcher with the Brooklyn and Los Angeles Dodgers and is best remembered in both Moriah and Brooklyn for being named the most valuable player of the 1955 World Series, when he pitched a shutout in Game 7 against the New York Yankees, helping the Dodgers win their first and only World Series title while in Brooklyn. He was honored by *Sport* magazine and given a two-seat red Corvette. He was also named *Sports Illustrated*'s Sportsman of the Year. Podres died in 2008 in Queensbury, New York. In 2012, Moriah residents erected this sign on Route 9N/22, on the southern entry to Port Henry, to honor his remarkable career. (Photograph by Janet Beebe Denney.)

Eight

LIFE ON THE LAKE

ICE BOATING, C. 1910. Ice boating is a demanding sport that is only feasible in early winter when lake ice has frozen solid but deep snows have not yet arrived. It was a cold and thrilling experience with strong winds and extremely fast speeds. This vessel was owned by a member of the Foote family, who lived on Lake Champlain. Note the boat's outrigger, which provided stability. (Courtesy of the Peggy Porter collection.)

Steamer Vermont, Lake Champlain

THE VERMONT. The 262-foot *Vermont III*, built in 1903, was the namesake of the first *Vermont* built in 1809. The *Vermont I* was the world's second viable commercial steamboat and the first steamboat on Lake Champlain. Early boats served towns on both sides of the lake and helped to link Port Henry to the commerce of Vermont.

THE CHATEAUGAY, C. 1900. The steamer *Chateaugay* was the first iron-hulled steamboat on Lake Champlain. Built in 1888, it was originally scheduled to run between Port Henry and Plattsburgh. After the *Ticonderoga* came into operation, the *Chateaugay* was used for excursions and special parties. It was refitted in 1925 as a car ferry and operated until 1939, when it was sold. The hull was cut into 20 sections and shipped by rail to Lake Winnepesaukee, New Hampshire, for reuse in another vessel.

100

FERRY SCHEDULE, 1892. Crossing at the lake's narrowest point, the steamer *G.R. Sherman* provided the quickest crossing of Lake Champlain. Fort Frederick was the ruin of a French fort built at Crown Point in the 1700s. During the French and Indian War, the British burned the houses on the Vermont side, leaving only the chimneys, thus the name Chimney Point.

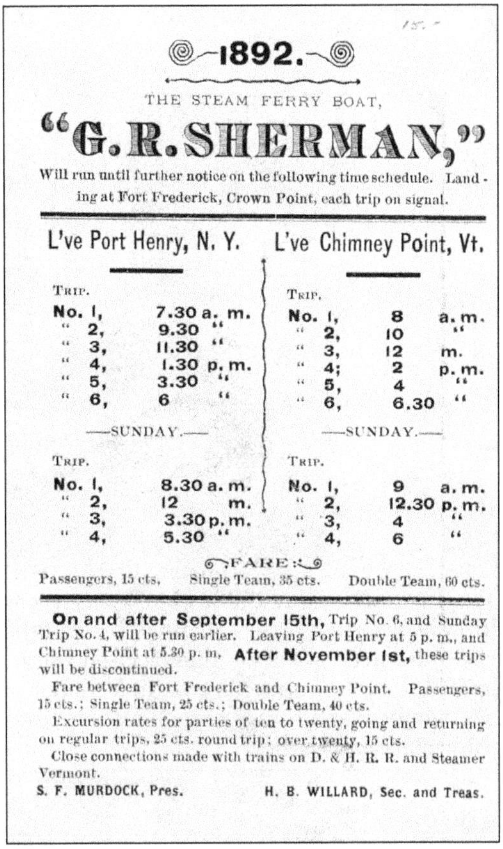

THE *G.R. SHERMAN*, C. 1890. In the 1800s, Lake Champlain towns were economically tied to the towns that could be reached directly by ferry. In 1890, the *G.R. Sherman*, pictured here, named for the Witherbee, Sherman & Company cofounder, was commissioned to Port Henry. It connected the village to Fort Frederick, New York, and Chimney Point, Vermont. Here, it is docked at Port Henry's pier by the Bay State furnaces, waiting for passengers to board. Its captain, Thomas E. Weatherwax, was widely known and respected. He captained the *Sherman* from its commissioning in 1890 until 1929, when it was replaced by the Lake Champlain Bridge. (Courtesy of the Anna Beebe collection.)

©~1892.~©

THE STEAM FERRY BOAT,

"**G. R. SHERMAN,**"

Will run until further notice on the following time schedule. Landing at Fort Frederick, Crown Point, each trip on signal.

L've Port Henry, N. Y.		L've Chimney Point, Vt.		
TRIP.		TRIP.		
No. I,	7.30 a. m.	No. I,	8	a. m.
" 2,	9.30 "	" 2,	10	"
" 3,	11.30 "	" 3,	12	m.
" 4,	1.30 p. m.	" 4;	2	p. m.
" 5,	3.30 "	" 5,	4	"
" 6,	6 "	" 6,	6.30	"
—SUNDAY.—		—SUNDAY.—		
TRIP.		TRIP.		
No. I,	8.30 a. m.	No. I,	9	a. m.
" 2,	12 m.	" 2,	12.30 p. m.	
" 3,	3.30 p. m.	" 3,	4	"
" 4,	5.30 "	" 4,	6	"

©~FARE:~©

Passengers, 15 cts.   Single Team, 35 cts.   Double Team, 60 cts.

On and after September 15th, Trip No. 6, and Sunday Trip No. 4, will be run earlier. Leaving Port Henry at 5 p. m., and Chimney Point at 5.30 p. m, **After November 1st,** these trips will be discontinued.

Fare between Fort Frederick and Chimney Point. Passengers, 15 cts.; Single Team, 25 cts.; Double Team, 40 cts.

Excursion rates for parties of ten to twenty, going and returning on regular trips, 25 cts. round trip; over twenty, 15 cts.

Close connections made with trains on D. & H. R. R. and Steamer Vermont.

S. F. MURDOCK, Pres.   H. B. WILLARD, Sec. and Treas.

THE *TICONDEROGA*, C. 1908. The *Ticonderoga* was built in the Shelburne shipyard in 1905–1906. In 1909, it ferried Pres. William Taft and other dignitaries around the lake. Operations were suspended in 1933, but business picked up during World War II, and it was put back into service. In 1951, the Shelburne Museum in Vermont purchased the vessel, and in 1954–1955, the boat made an overland voyage to the museum. Today, visitors to the museum can view a film about this remarkable journey.

CAPT. GRANT EDSON, C. 1910. Somewhat of a celebrity in the Port Henry area, Capt. Grant Edson was the only Moriah native to ever become a captain on the Lake Champlain steamships, a prestigious rank that required much expertise. Edson captained the *Ticonderoga* for many years, as well as the *Chateaugay* at times. Notice the pens in his jacket pocket and the four stripes on his sleeves. The life ring behind him shows that he was on the *Chateaugay* in this photograph. The wooden deck chairs with straw seats were typical of steamboats in the early 1900s. (Courtesy of the Peggy Porter collection.)

WITHERBEE, SHERMAN & COMPANY POWER PLANT, C. 1910. Witherbee, Sherman & Company shaped Moriah in many ways, including with the state-of-the-art power plant above. Built in 1908 on the lakefront below their headquarters, the power plant was sited for easy coal delivery by barge. On the left, the steamer *Vermont*, which connected Port Henry with towns around Lake Champlain, comes in to dock. To the right, note the elegant wooden boathouse with a porch and balconies, which must have offered fine viewing of regattas and other lake events.

ROCK CUT NEAR LAKE CHAMPLAIN FOR THE RAILROAD, C. 1900 POSTCARD. The Adirondacks and Moriah reflect a rich geological history, with surface rock that is millions of years old. For the builders of the Delaware & Hudson Railroad, this geology posed a significant engineering challenge as they tried to create a relatively level track alignment. Many of these cutaways were blasted, with the extra rock hauled to fill in other areas. (Courtesy of the Anna Beebe collection.)

CEDAR POINT HOUSE, C. 1900. Cedar Point House was built as a lodge in the 1880s on South Main Street in Port Henry. It was electrified in 1900 by running an electric line across the road from the Cedar Point furnace. Peter and Helen Adamowicz were the proprietors of the successful restaurant and inn for more than 30 years. Home-cooked meals on white linen tablecloths were served in the dining room to both locals and visitors.

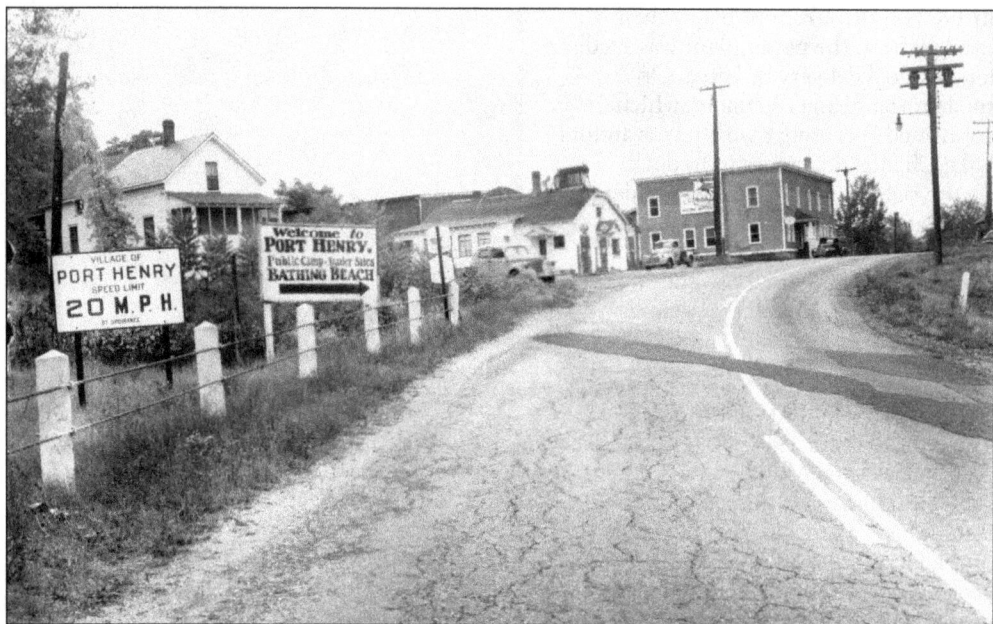

SOUTH APPROACH INTO PORT HENRY, C. 1940. Approaching Port Henry from the south, visitors were welcomed to the village and directed to the bathing beach. The campground and bathing beach are still on the north side of the village, and this curve on Route 9N looks much the same today.

COUGHLIN'S, C. 1930 POSTCARD. Four miles north of Port Henry, Coughlin's Midway Bathing Beach provided an excellent stopping place. They served meals and had a beach for overnight and day guests. Located on the shores of Lake Champlain, it offered a view of the lake for diners. Many Port Henry adults today fondly remember going to Coughlin's Beach in the summer and getting ice cream and hot dogs at its snack bar.

COUGHLIN'S "OVERNITE CAMP," C. 1930 POSTCARD. Here is another view of the Coughlin operation in its prime, when they served meals at all hours, ran a beach, offered campsites, and rented cabins. With the rise of automobile travel and tourism, such campgrounds and "cottage courts" met the new needs of travelers, who could now venture far from home with the independence of their own car. Unlike the Lee House, which was built in the age of train travel and had its own carriage to bring guests from Port Henry's depot, Coughlin's offered a much more informal family experience for guests, who came from all directions. (Courtesy of the Peggy Porter collection.)

ICE FISHING ON LAKE CHAMPLAIN, 1968. Taken from Spring Street in Port Henry in the winter of 1968, this photograph shows the popularity of ice fishing throughout much of the 1900s. Clusters of ice shanties are gathered near good fishing spots out on the ice. At one time, many fish, including smelt, were boxed in ice and shipped by train to New York City and other destinations. In this photograph, the Witherbee, Sherman & Company power plant is a prominent landmark. It was demolished in 1973.

CHAMP DAY, C. 1960. Dating back to the Native Americans and the first voyages of Samuel de Champlain 400 years ago on the lake that bears his name, locals have recorded "Champ sightings." Port Henry is particularly fond of Champ, with an annual Champ Day and a roadside rest area with a sign listing major Champ sightings. Today, many people claim to have seen the local sea monster. (Courtesy of the Bernadette Trow collection.)

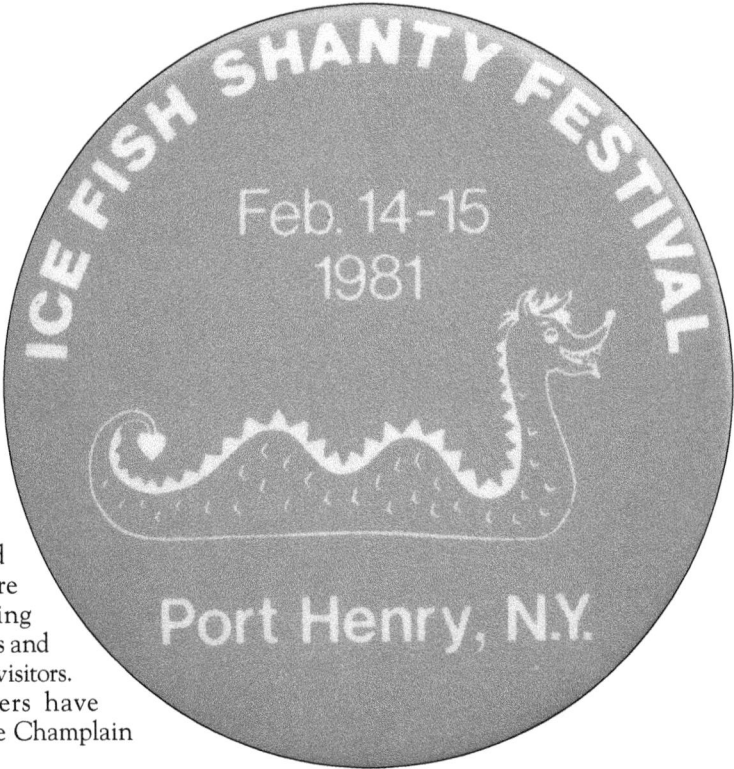

ICE SHANTY FESTIVAL PIN, 1981. As recently as the 1980s, ice fishing was a vibrant winter lake activity in Port Henry. This pin is from the annual Ice Shanty Festival that was held each February, when ice thickness and fishing conditions were at their prime. A smiling Champ, with two humps and a curving tail, welcomes visitors. Recent warmer winters have prevented much of Lake Champlain from freezing over.

1929 BRIDGE. The original Lake Champlain Bridge opened in 1929. Future president Franklin D. Roosevelt, who was the governor of New York at the time, attended the opening with dignitaries from Vermont. The bridge was built high enough so that the steamer *Ticonderoga* could pass under it. This view looks northwest toward Port Henry.

NEW LAKE CHAMPLAIN BRIDGE. The arch for the new bridge was built at Velez Marina in Port Henry by Flatiron. The arch was floated across the lake in August 2011, just a few days before Hurricane Irene ravaged the Lake Champlain area. Floating the arch to the bridge site took many hours and was witnessed by a great number of spectators. It was then hoisted into place by steel cables. The arch has an elegance reminiscent of the 1929 bridge, but there are now much wider side lanes for bicycles and walkers. At night, the bridge is dramatically illuminated with contemporary LED lighting. (Photograph by Janet Beebe Denney.)

BRIDGE TOLL BOOTH, C. 1935 POSTCARD. The Lake Champlain Bridge opened as a toll bridge in 1929. Seen on this postcard are the toll keeper's booth and house. The toll was taken off in 1987. The newly restored tollhouse is now an information center for Vermont and New York, with historical exhibits and artifacts about the history of Crown Point and the first and second bridges at the site.

THE MORNINGSIDE INN, C. 1930. Fisherman, hikers, and boaters could choose from a variety of places to stay in Port Henry. Seen here is the Morningside Inn, which was built in the 1920s and provided rooms and meals. Ben Collins purchased the motel in 1946 and made many improvements to the establishment, which is still operating today.

110

VACATION AT PORT HENRY. For generations, Port Henry has promoted its superb beaches and fishing. Indeed, Port Henry has more public lakefront than almost any other village on Lake Champlain. This brochure from around 1940 shows many photographs of the water and includes the slogan "Where you Look and Linger."

Vacation at

Port Henry

IN THE ADIRONDACKS
NEW YORK

Where You Look and Linger

SUNRISE MOTOR COURT. Located about four miles north of Port Henry on Route 9N, the Sunrise Motor Court was typical of many family resorts and roadside lodgings of the 1930s. Long before large chain hotels, these "courts" gave tourists their own cottage and parking spot. Today, Route 9N is still used for recreational travel for drivers of cars, RVs, motorbikes, and bicyclists. Running through downtown Port Henry, Route 9N is part of the Lakes to Locks Passage National Scenic Byway. (Courtesy of the Anna Beebe collection.)

SUNRISE MOTOR COURT – ROUTE 22 & 9 ... . NORTH --
PORT HENRY N. Y.

111

BIRD'S-EYE VIEW OF CONVENT HILL AND LAKE CHAMPLAIN. This postcard shows a rare view of the village and the railroad from the north. Notice the openness of much of the foreground. The small harbor along the lake was eventually filled with mining tailings to create Port Henry's village beach and campground.

LAKE VIEW. This photograph shows the blend of industrial, commercial, and recreational activities along Port Henry's waterfront in the late 1800s. The boats to the right appear to be a small launch and a sailboat. To the left stands a wooden rail trestle for the loading of ore onto barges.

Nine

LIVING AND CAMPING IN THE ADIRONDACKS

THE OVERLOOK, C. 1900 POSTCARD. Home to a distinctive style of architecture, the Adirondacks and Port Henry have a rich architectural history of camps built of local wood and stone and designed to immerse 19th-century families in nature. North of Port Henry on Lake Champlain, the Overlook was a small camp suspended far out over the water. Such quirky and delightful design is found in many North County summer homes and camps. (Courtesy of the Peggy Porter collection.)

CAMP WOODALL TRAIL, C. 1920 POSTCARD. The Port Henry area is still home to many small camps and summer homes connected by winding dirt lanes. Set along streams and small lakes such as Lincoln Pond, these simple wood-frame cottages with vertical log siding were often owned by residents of Port Henry, who would camp out in the woods for the summer just a few miles from their homes in the village. (Courtesy of the Anna Beebe collection.)

BROWNIE LAKESHORE CAMP, C. 1920 POSTCARD. Many families gave their summer camps playful names. The Brownie camp, seen here, provided everything needed for a rustic summer at the lake. A log-framed porch is ideal for dining, reading, and napping. Upstairs most likely is a bedroom cooled by nighttime cross-breezes through screened windows. Just off the porch, a small handmade bench is crafted between two trees. (Courtesy of the Anna Beebe collection.)

4-Leaf Clover Camp, c. 1910 Postcard. This is another example of playful camp architecture in the Port Henry area. Built with cement slabs and wood taken from the former sets of the Arctic City film studio in Port Henry, 4-Leaf Camp and its neighbors in the Woodall Trail area north of Port Henry took advantage of local materials. The hipped central roof flanked by octagonal pavilions lends this unusual building a kind of circus-like quality. Children must have loved its intimate scale and the front porch so close to the water's edge. The pine-branch front railing and roof brackets are typical of camps throughout the Adirondacks. (Courtesy of the Peggy Porter collection.)

a Bus at Jiger's Camp
Port Henry, N.Y.

EARLY TOURIST BUS IN PORT HENRY, C. 1930. After World War I, many tourists began to visit the Adirondacks and Port Henry by motor coach. This postcard shows a tour bus from the Albany-Cohoes Bus Line parked at Jiger's Camp, a small resort four miles north of Port Henry. Buses operated on regular routes, connecting towns and resorts. Other buses, such as this one operated by F. Bohl Tours, took tourists on scenic drives into the mountains. (Courtesy of the Anna Beebe collection.)

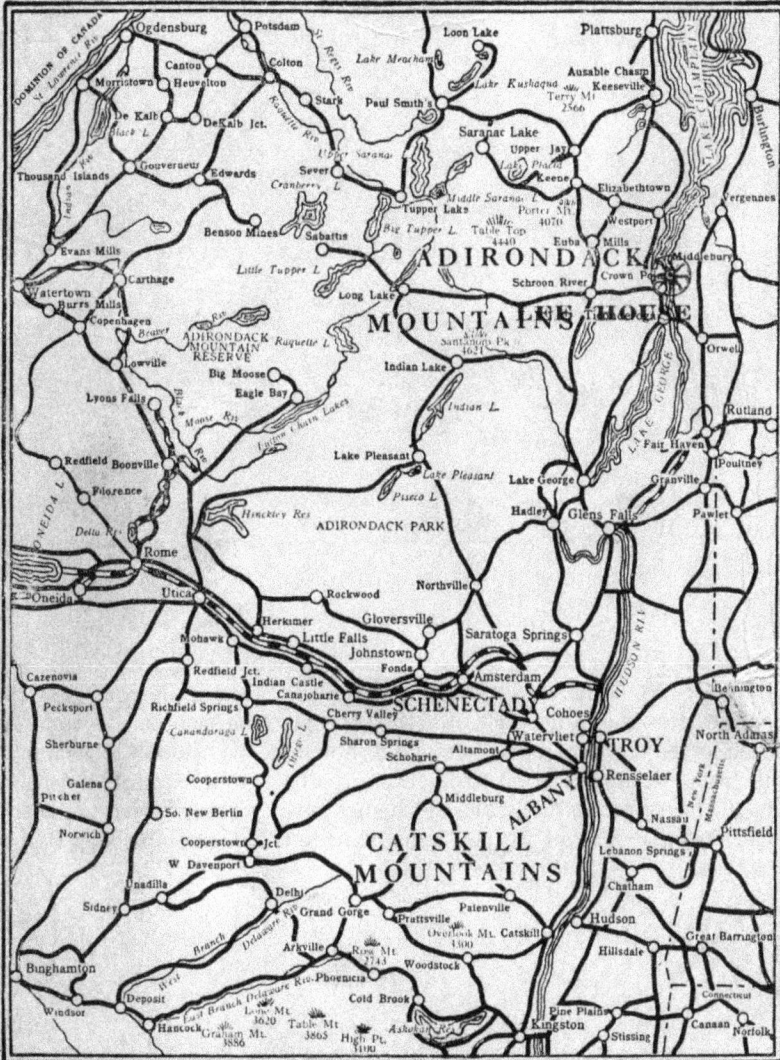

THE LEE HOUSE,
PORT HENRY, N. Y.

Copyrighted by The Bullard Company, Boston

JOHN A. McNULTY, PROP.

ROAD MAP POSTCARD, C. 1935. As a gateway to the Adirondacks, Port Henry and its well-known hotel, the Lee House, became a destination for motorists after the 1920s. This postcard is a "map showing best automobile routes." Port Henry and Lake Champlain are shown to the upper right. At the center are Lake Placid and the High Peaks. Albany and Troy are to the south with the Catskill Mountains.

ADIRONDACK FARM AND TAILINGS PILE. The town of Moriah extends from the shores of Lake Champlain upward into the Adirondacks. On the lower plateaus near the lake, some family farms have continued for generations. This photograph shows one of them, on Edgemont Road, with a tailings pile from mining operations rising up in the background and the High Peaks in the distance. On fall and spring mornings, Moriah's higher elevations are often covered in new snow or frost while the flatter lands along the lake remain green. (Photograph by Janet Beebe Denney.)

THE KING AND QUEEN OF THE OLYMPICS, 1932. Port Henry native Lucille Hickey (right) was crowned queen of the 1932 Winter Olympics. On her left, holding a scepter, is John Shea of Lake Placid, who served as king. Hickey was one of many contestants from throughout upstate New York for this regal honor. She later married Jim McNulty and ran the Lee House with him for many years. Today, Lake Placid remains the US Olympic Team's official winter sports training center. (Courtesy of the Mary Gilbo collection.)

FIRE TOWER ON BELFRY MOUNTAIN. In the early 1950s, Republic Steel constructed a road to this tower, which was built between 1913 and 1915, for the purpose of placing fire sirens on the mountain. It operated as a fire tower until the 1960s. Today, the tower is a popular hiking spot. From this tower, on Belfry Mountain, visitors can look west to the High Peaks and south to Lake Champlain. In the spring, birders can witness the migration of the raptors that pass through on their way to Canada.

AERIAL VIEW OF PORT HENRY CCC CAMP, 1934. Located near today's Moriah Central School, the Port Henry Civilian Conservation Corps (CCC) camp operated from the end of 1933 until January 1936. Enrollees signed up for six months and earned $30 per week. The federal government sent $25 to the enrollee's family, and the enrollee received $5. Because much of forest-fire prevention involved the building of roads, fire watchtowers, and firebreaks, CCC enrollees helped bring modern forest management practices to the Adirondacks. One of the New Deal's most popular programs, the CCC trained young men in such skills as forestry, firefighting, and stonework. In the Adirondacks, enrollees built trails, roads, and campsites and planted millions of trees. At its peak, the CCC had more than half a million enrollees across the country. (Courtesy of the Anna Beebe collection.)

PORT HENRY CCC CAMP. For more than two years, Port Henry was home to the 203rd Company of the CCC. At left is the seal for the 203rd on a green and yellow pennant. The US Army supervised CCC camps, which generally had 200 enrollees—men aged 18 to 25. The CCC helped keep many families alive during the depth of the Depression and trained young men in lifelong skills, including construction, forestry, and even journalism, as demonstrated by the camp newspaper seen below. The enrollees contributed their own stories to the newspaper, and many of the young men also took writing, math, and other high school classes while in the CCC. The young men received nutritious food, uniforms, and medical care. The program ended in 1942 with the rise of World War II. (Below, courtesy of the Peggy Porter collection.)

Adirondack Range
203ᵈ Company CCC Camp P-74

VOL. I, NO. 7   PORT HENRY, N. Y.   DECEMBER, 193_

COMMANDING OFFICER'S COLUMN

HOLIDAY LEAVE

LEADERS AND LEADERSHIP
(By Harvey Napier)

PEST CONTROL
Capt. Ray N. Cooley

N. Y. TIMES CITES CAMP

GROUP SHOT AT CCC CAMP. This group photograph of the Port Henry CCC camp was taken from the center segment of a much wider Circuit photograph. Popular in the early 1900s, the Circuit camera used large roll film, usually 8 inches to 12 inches high. The photographer wound up the large camera so that it rotated on its tripod. The film would roll through as the camera slowly swiveled. By posing in a large semicircle, the subjects could achieve the illusion of being in a straight line, with everyone in focus. This shot shows the young enrollees in their army-issue uniforms. In the background are older men who may have been local master tradesmen serving as teachers. The men on the right are Army officers. The board-and-batten siding on the camp superintendent's office was typical of CCC buildings.

HUNTING PARTY AT ELK LAKE, 1930. Hunting and fishing trips have long been part of life in the Adirondacks. For more than a century, before ice-fishing season began, groups of men from Port Henry and Moriah's villages traveled to nearby lakes and mountains for hunting. Taken in 1930 at Elk Lake, this photograph shows a group of smiling hunters enjoying beers after a day in the field. The man sitting on the far left in the first row is Jim McNulty, an owner of the Lee House and the future husband of Lucille Hickey, who was crowned queen of the 1932 Winter Olympics at Lake Placid. The man smoking a pipe in the first row is Ernest Hamner, their guide. Hanging in the center of the photograph, the handsome stag appears to have a more stoic attitude about the day's events. (Courtesy of the Peggy Porter collection.)

125

OUT FOR A DRIVE, C. 1925. The invention of the automobile and the popularity of motoring brought a new wave of tourism to the Adirondacks and Port Henry. In this snapshot, a traveling group poses behind the windshield. Dressed in hats for protection against sun and wind, they are likely traveling north on Route 9N, a beautiful drive between lakes and mountains. (Courtesy of the Anna Beebe collection.)

BIBLIOGRAPHY

Farrell, Patrick F. *Through the Light Hole: A Saga of Adirondack Mines and Men.* Utica, NY: North Country Books, 1996.

Rosenquist, Valerie Beth. "The Iron Ore Eaters: A Portrait of the Mining Community of Moriah, New York" (PhD diss., Duke University, 1987).

Warner, Dr. Charles B. and C. Eleanor Hall. *History of Port Henry, N.Y.* Port Henry, NY: First Presbyterian Church, 1931.

Visit us at
arcadiapublishing.com

www.ingramcontent.com/pod-product-compliance
Lightning Source LLC
Chambersburg PA
CBHW050702110426
42813CB00007B/2062